# Dark Psychology Secrets and Manipulation

---

*A Speed Guide to Analyze Human Personality Types and the Signs of a Toxic Person. Stop Being Manipulated Mastering Mind Control, Persuasion & NLP Techniques.*

---

## Brandon Robinson

# Table of Contents


TABLE OF CONTENTS ................................................................3

INTRODUCTION ...................................................................5

CHAPTER 1:  MANIPULATION AND DARK PSYCHOLOGY ...................7

CHAPTER 2:  THE DIFFERENCE BETWEEN MANIPULATION AND PERSUASION.................................................................24

CHAPTER 3:  THE DARK TRIAD.................................................32

CHAPTER 4:  MANIPULATOR BEHAVIORAL AND CHARACTER TRAITS 48

CHAPTER 5:  MIND CONTROL AND MIND GAMES..........................54

CHAPTER 6:  PROFILE OF A MANIPULATOR IN DETAIL ...............77

CHAPTER 7:  HOW TO DEAL WITH A MANIPULATOR?...................99

CHAPTER 8:  ARE MANIPULATORS AWARE OF THEIR ACTIONS ..........109

CHAPTER 9:  EMOTIONAL MANIPULATION IN A RELATIONSHIP .........113

CHAPTER 10:  WHAT MANIPULATORS TEND TO DO? .....................135

CHAPTER 11:  MANIPULATION TACTICS ...................................144

CHAPTER 12:  FAVORITE VICTIMS ........................................156

CHAPTER 13:  BODY LANGUAGE ..........................................163

CHAPTER 14:  SECRETS TO PROTECT YOURSELF .......................178

CONCLUSION..................................................................209

# Introduction

Manipulation is dangerous, but when it is seen in a different light, it can become a healthy influence. If you are able to be a persuasive individual and not only get what you want, but fulfill the needs of others as well, then it will become easier for you to be able to get the things that you desire the most in life.

Rather than always doing things you don't enjoy, being the "yes man," or letting people take advantage of your good nature, you can become just as influential as the people who have tried to control you previously.

You might even be at a point where you fear manipulation altogether. Why would you want to do something to others that has actually caused you grief in the past? This kind of thinking is because we have only been aware of the negative types of manipulation. Not only that, but it is important to ensure we have the tools to understand how to get these things.

With that information in the bag, let's begin our journey into the world of mind-control and manipulation. There are going to be some dry areas in the reading. The book Gods require this from time to time. However, most will be very lighthearted, informative, and enjoyable to read. So, without further ado, let's get to reading and let the learning begin!

# Chapter 1:
# Manipulation and Dark Psychology

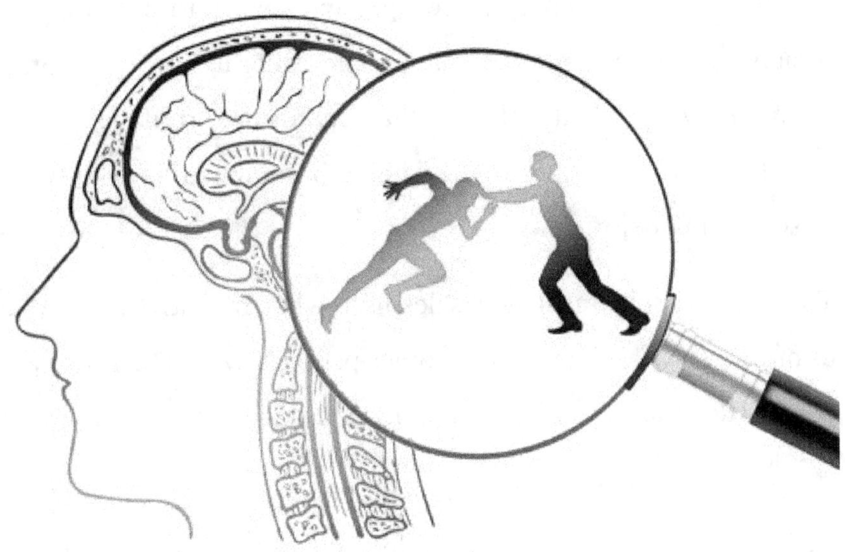

## WHAT IS MANIPULATION?

Manipulation can be defined as a social influence that has the potential to change the attitude or reasoning of a subject, employing a deceptive, abusive, or underhanded strategy. The manipulator's aim is to work to enhance their personal interest, usually at the expense of the subject(s), as such, most of their methods are considered as being deceptive, devious, abusive, and intended to exploit the subject. Although in itself, social influence is not always negative, when a subject or group of people are being manipulated, it has the potential to cause harm to those involved.

Social influence, such as a teenager inducted into a culture or a society to interact with different people either at home or work, is admirable. Any social influence that regards the privilege and right of individuals to decide, without being intimidated, is usually seen as something helpful.

Then again, social influence is despised when people beguile others to maneuver their way against other people's will. The impact can be very destructive and generally looked down upon as very weak.

Emotional or psychological manipulation is also a type of influence and pressure. Hence, numerous elements can be incorporated into this type of brainwashing and bullying. For example, harassing and mental conditioning. Generally, people will consider this to be damaging and misleading, although people who manipulate others to do their will, do it at the expense of their selfish interest to gain dominance using every means possible. The manipulator will work through cruel ways to connive with people and pressurize their subject to succumb to their will to achieve their aim.

People who manipulate others use several means such as brainwashing, dark psychology and bullying techniques to compel people to believe them. The subjects of the manipulator are not willing to comply most times, but because they have been blackmailed, they have no option to disagree. These manipulators lack conscience and sensitivity towards others; as a result, they find their act very pleasing. Since they aim to achieve their objective without being bothered about who was harmed during the process, they will apply all tactics available to get their expected result.

Furthermore, manipulative individuals are hesitant to get into a relationship because of an inferiority complex. They see themselves as an outcast amidst others and being uncomfortable to associate freely. People of this tendency find it difficult to engage in meaningful activities. They are handicapped in taking responsibility into their own hands in their actions, issues, and life. Rather, they will rely on other people through various manipulative tactics to achieve their aim. Manipulators use different tactics to control the mind and exercise dominance over others.

Emotional blackmail is one of the most used strategies, making the victim act through sympathy or guilt. These two emotions are the most important in every human life. It's a process whereby the manipulator tries to impress the victim through several means to be able to get the desired result. hey choose guilt or sympathy to coerce their subject and make them comply with their will. Then, from here, the manipulator will assume total control of the person, using the sympathy or guilt they create to constrain others to enable themselves to attain success.

Often, the manipulator doesn't do it alone; he does it with the assistance of others in order not to go out of a plan. He may devise a means to create sympathy, such as missing out on a very important gathering e.g. wedding anniversary or funeral, using the sympathy or guilt emotions.

They adopt an emotional blackmail strategy in conjunction with an abusive strategy which is still the most effective of them. This is also known as crazy-making. This abusive or crazy-making strategy is used to cripple the confidence of a victim to the extent that they may be uncertain of their sanity.

Often, the manipulator may devise a means of a passive-aggressive method to bring out crazy-making. They could even show compassion on the victim at their presence with their mouth, but carry something else within their heart that could be more devastating. They work tirelessly to sabotage a victim, but if caught in the act, they will devise a thousand means to deny it, such as justification, rationalization and deception, just to be freed.

The commonest act of psychological manipulators is that they shy away from something that may be beneficial to others, whether they have it or not. They don't put people into consideration. Their minds are wired with manipulative devices and as a result, they lack feelings of sympathy toward others. They see helping or assisting as not part of their priority, which makes it very hard to stop them from their destructive actions.

However, people may find them unworthy to deal with, due to their prior manipulative characteristics. This has hindered their ability to keep friends and earn trust. Although in the form of relationships, the problems work hand-in-hand. The manipulator may never find their fellow worthy; the fellow may also feel unsafe in the hands of the manipulator. This lack of trust will hinder their emotional connection.

## HOW TO UTILIZE MANIPULATION

Manipulation is a technique used by everyone at some point in life. If you think about it, you start learning to manipulate as a small child. For example, you start taking on extra chores and a week or two later, you ask for a new toy. Your parents feel compelled to give it to you since you have been helping so much. This same strategy works in adulthood too. There are numerous financial and emotional benefits that come with properly using the different manipulation techniques.

Manipulation essentially plays on people's emotions. However, to be effective, you need to be able to successfully do this and be able to read people. Several techniques will allow you to do both of these. Once you are good at both, you will find it much easier to get what you want every time that you need something.

## **Fear and Relief**

This is a common manipulation technique that you have used at some point without even realizing it. This involves using another person's fears to get them to do something for you. You essentially cause some type of fear and let it build. Once the person is getting to the peak of their emotion, you relieve that fear. At this point, they are vulnerable and much more likely to do something for you.

This is a technique that is used by employers regularly. They make it seem like a person might lose their job, then eventually reassure them and ask that employee to do something. Of course, the employee does it because they feel they have to do it to keep their job.

## Reading Body Language

When you can determine a person's state of mind, it is easier to control it. Sure, you can ask them what they are thinking, but more often than not, they will not be honest. However, you cannot fake body language. If you can read body language, you will know exactly what a person is thinking. For example, you are trying to persuade someone to give you money. Their words are saying "no," but their body language shows that you are breaking them down. As long as you can read this body language, you will know that you can push further and get the money that you need.

You want to see how they are holding their posture if they are still or moving and where they are looking when they are talking to you. All of this tells you exactly what they are thinking, despite what they are saying.

## Guilty Approach

This is a manipulation technique that humans have been using on each other since the dawn of time. When you make a person feel guilty about something, you make them vulnerable, and vulnerable people are easier to persuade. It is best to use this technique on people you know on a personal level. This is because you can find something that you know will induce some guilt. This technique makes it possible to slowly plant your desires. Then, when you suggest an idea, they tend to go with the flow on a subconscious level.

## Use Your Looks

Humans, whether they admit it or not, tend to be shallow when it comes to looks. This is just a fact and even if you recognize this trait in yourself, you cannot help it. If you tend to be good looking by society's standards, it is much easier to persuade people to do things for you.

Several studies were done that looked at this. In the studies, they would send out people who were attractive and unattractive by society's standards. Both groups of people would ask strangers for small favors, such as borrowing a dollar for public transportation or using their cellphone. Those that were deemed attractive were far more successful in getting what they wanted, and they got it simply because of their outward appearance.

Just ensure that, when you use your looks to persuade, you present a total package. This means that you want to use inclusive body language and confidence. Make the person you are trying to persuade feel special and they will eat out of your hands.

## Play the Victim

This is another common manipulation technique that really works. When you play the victim, you essentially make people feel sorry for you. When people feel this way, it is a natural human instinct for them to want to correct what they did to make you feel bad. When they are in this vulnerable state, you can essentially make them do anything. Now, this technique will not work on all people. You have to choose those that are naturally more vulnerable and less tough. The tougher people usually will not fall for the victim act, so use this technique wisely.

## Prey on Their Feelings

This technique can work on all people, but is easiest with those who are already emotionally vulnerable. With this technique, you essentially make people fall for you to get them to do what you need. When a person falls for someone, they are less likely to make rational decisions. Instead, they make choices on an emotional level. When someone is thinking with their emotions, they are much easier to control.

Now, this is certainly a more advanced manipulation technique. To use it successfully, you have to first get a hold of your own feelings and emotions. You essentially need to be able to detach yourself, and this will not work well on people you have actual feelings for. Look for those that you need in your life, but those that if they leave, it will not hurt you on an emotional level. For example, choose a coworker who can do things for you at work, so you do not have to work as hard. Just ensure you have a pre-existing friendship, but not one so deep that you feel emotionally connected. Make them fall for you and then use this to your advantage.

## **Bribery**

This is one of the oldest manipulation techniques in the book because it is almost always effective. When someone feels as though they are being rewarded for helping you, they are almost always going to help.

For example, you do not feel like doing the finance report at work. Find someone who can do it, ease into the conversation, and then offer them lunch if they will do the report. Make sure that you are confident when you are asking, since it is harder to say "no" to a person who is smiling and confident. Keep your tone neutral and make sure to follow through with your bribe. Once this works once, it will be much easier to persuade that person in the future without even having to bribe them.

## HOW TO USE DARK PSYCHOLOGY TO MANIPULATE OTHERS?

People around us may use dark psychology tactics every day to manipulate, influence, persuade and intimidate us to take advantage and get what they want. As you will get to know, dark psychology includes the science and art of mind control and manipulation, whereas psychology is different as it is the study of human behavior and our actions, interactions and thoughts. Some people get confused and don't know the difference between psychology and dark psychology. However, if you want to manipulate others, you need to know how to use dark psychology.

Dark psychology, in particular, will look specifically at the psychology of people that have a very specific personality type.

In particular, we are looking at those who are Machiavellian, narcissistic, sadistic and psychopathic. These people tend to be among the most dangerous that you can encounter, and they will have no qualms about using and abusing other people.

However, there is much to learn from this personality type—if you can come to understand this personality type and the tactics that are commonly used, you will be able to emulate them without the threat or harm that may otherwise go along with them.

In particular, this book will be looking at the behaviors of those with dark personality types. From there, the duration of the book will be spent studying the behavior of those specific personality types.

Dark psychology assumes that when people behave in abusive manners, using techniques like manipulation and deception, it almost always has a reason.

We will look at those reasons and applications as well, learning what it is that makes these tools so attractive to monsters in human clothing who are willing to wield them.

You will see exactly why people behave in ways that are abusive or evil, how they come to the realization that justifies the abuse in their minds, and how they are able to overcome the empathy and compassion that usually prevent people from behaving in such abusive manners.

We will look at several of the most commonly used techniques of abusive personality types and from there, we will spend time discussing how several of them can be used in a wider context, allowing for their usage during day-to-day interactions.

Instead of manipulating someone to abuse them, you can look into how to use the same skills to help persuade and guide people toward whatever they need to do.

We will also look into how these particular tactics impact the person that is being subjected to them. Some of these techniques work through instilling feelings in other people, knowing that emotions are incredibly motivating.

Others work through accessing the unconscious mind and suggesting certain behaviors. Others still work through acts of deception.

Understanding dark psychology will not only enable you to understand the actions of personality types such as the narcissist, the Machiavellian and the psychopath but also be able to combat it.

You will be able to avoid falling for their tactics if you know what the tactics are. This means that learning to think like the darkest personality types is imperative—when you can think like them, you can identify them.

## DIFFERENT MANIPULATIVE PERSONALITIES

Manipulators have perfected the art of trickery. They may seem reasonable and genuine, but often it's just a cover; it's a way of drawing you in and pulling you into a connection before they reveal their hidden colors.

Manipulators are not really invested in you, but use you as a tool that helps them to acquire charge and therefore you are a reluctant member. As you'll acknowledge, they have many ways to do this. They often end up taking what you say or do and wiggle it around, so that what you've said and done will hardly be recognizable to you. They'll try to mislead you, and perhaps even make you feel like you're crazy. They stretch the facts, and if it helps their end they may succumb to lying.

## **Deceitful Personalities**

The victim role can be portrayed by dishonest people, making you appear to be the one who created a crisis they began but never accepted accountability for. They can act as passive-aggressive or pleasant for one minute and stand-offish the next, keeping you speculating and preying on your fears and worries. Often, they do make you nervous. Also, they can be highly violent and brutal, resorting to character insults and criticism, savage in their quest to get what they want. They are bullying and threatening and will not let go till they wear you down.

Manipulators possess the following traits, so when one catches your eye, you'll know what to look out for. Knowing these underlying concepts of operation can help safeguard you from getting drawn into a deceitful relationship. Staying vigilant and connected with what you know is true about yourself and anticipating what is to come will allow you to prevent a dispute and preserve your own dignity.

1. Manipulative individuals often lack understanding of how they involve someone to construct those situations, or they genuinely feel that their method of coping with a problem is the right option, as it ensures their desires are being fulfilled and that's all that counts. Inevitably, all the circumstances and partnerships are for them, and it just doesn't matter what others say, hear and want:

    "Controllers, bullies, and manipulators are not challenging themselves. They aren't asking themselves whether they are the problem. They always conclude others are the problem."

2.  A manipulator shuns accountability for their own actions by accusing others of triggering them. It is not because dishonest people do not recognize what responsibility is. They do; a dishonest person clearly finds nothing immoral with failing to accept accountability for their acts, even though they force you to take responsibility for yours. They can eventually seek to get you to assume accountability for fulfilling their needs, leaving no place to satisfy yours.

3.  Manipulators do not understand borders. They are ruthless in pursuing whatever they want and have little consideration as to who gets caught along the way.

    They're not worried about crowding your space — physically, mentally, socially or religiously. They clearly have no understanding or just don't care about what private space and individuality mean. They can be compared to a parasite - this is mostly an appropriate relationship in the natural environment. However, in an individual interaction, feeding off others at their cost is depleting, draining, diminishing and demeaning.

4.  Manipulative people prey on our sensibilities, interpersonal sensitivity and, in particular, conscience. They know they're going to have a decent chance to draw you into a friendship because you're loving, sensitive, compassionate and, of course, you want to support them. At first, they will care for your goodwill and generosity, always thanking you for

being the amazing individual that you are. But over time, praise for these attributes will lessen since you are being used to serve someone who doesn't truly care for you. They just really care what you can offer them.

5.  Never spend your energy attempting to justify who you are to those who are dedicated to misunderstanding you. When someone doesn't see you, don't sit around waiting until they do. You don't have to make it your task to make them appreciate and understand you — they are not interested in you as an individual.

6.  If you'd like a simple means of identifying manipulators from emphatic individuals, pay close attention to how they talk about others to you. Frequently, they will discuss you behind your back the same way they speak about someone else to you. They are masters of "triangulation"—creating situations and complexities that facilitate suspense, competition and envy, and promoting and fostering disharmony.

7.  Describe individuals by their acts and you'll never be deceived by their words. Always keep in mind that what an individual says and does are two very distinct aspects. Watch somebody else carefully, without finding excuses for them – usually what you're seeing is what you get.

8.  Investigate what you understand on a regular basis. We don't do this sufficiently. As life progresses, our perceptions

and opinions may change, and we need to understand how these shifting ideas impact us. If we're not sure what we understand, it's all too easy to let somebody else who is sure that their views are right — not just for them but for you as well — to try to influence your thought process.

9.  If an individual makes as much exertion to be a nice person as they do to pretend to be one, they might even be a good person in reality.

This is an important truth: Our initial contact and perspective of someone heavily color our growing connection with them. If we grasped from the outset that an individual is not who they appear to be and is only hiding behind a facade of what appears to be culturally acceptable behavior, then maybe we would be more cautious about getting involved.

If it comes to manipulating human beings, there is no stronger tool than lies. Since, you know, people live through ideologies and values can be twisted, the only thing that matters is the ability to exploit ideologies.

# Chapter 2:
# The Difference Between Manipulation And Persuasion

## PERSUASION VS. MANIPULATION

The line between persuasion and manipulation is so thin that it often gets blurry. Distinguishing these two concepts can often be difficult, especially depending on the circumstances and your own perspective as an individual. Persuasion and manipulation are alike in that in both cases there is someone trying to influence the decisions and behaviors of another. The key distinction between the two is that manipulation is seen to be highly driven by self-interest where one party is willing to go through any length to benefit themselves, including putting others in harm's way.

Persuasion, on the other hand, is the nicer cousin of manipulation - there is a desire to influence for self-interest, but there is often a line drawn to mark boundaries. Persuasion is the more ethical way to go about it, as many will argue. When all's said and done, however, the two concepts seem to intertwine, especially depending on the techniques used to achieve either of them.

People always have different ideas of what words mean, but to be successful in manipulation and persuasion, you need to know the different ways these terms are understood as well as what we mean when using them in this book. In common speech, persuasion is considered a neutral word; of course, someone can be persuaded to do something that helps the persuader and not themselves, but the word itself does not imply that. Manipulation, on the other hand, tends to imply ill intention of the manipulator.

The ethics of manipulation and persuasion are a topic we have explored throughout these pages, but know that, for our purposes, persuasion is changing someone's beliefs, while manipulation is changing someone's actions. This is easy to remember, because NLP involves the neural pathways for both language (belief) and programming (action).

If you want your subject to change their behavior, you have to get them to change their thinking about their behavior. They are a thinking person just like you are, and while they have mental shortcuts that can get in the way (just like they can for you), your subject is entirely capable of talking through their judgment calls with you. In a conversation with you, they can come to re-evaluate their actions, and if you go through the conversation the right way, you will have the opportunity to convince them to change.

When it comes to manipulation, there is a slight difference from persuasion. The difference is that at some points, it is, in fact, the right thing to ask them to change their behavior directly. Now, you don't want to pull this out as your first move. This is something you build up to after a long conversation — after you accomplish steps zero and one, just as you do for persuasion. But the big difference between changing someone's ideas and changing their behaviors is here in step two: more often than not, you should directly tell them what you think they should do differently.

When NLP newcomers learn this at first, they are totally taken aback. They think, how could I possibly be told to tell them directly to change their behavior? But if you think through it a little longer, it makes sense. What is the difference between belief and behavior? Persuasion changes belief by getting close to someone's mind and changing what is in there, and manipulation is getting closer to their mind and changing what is in there, too.

But with manipulation, there is the added hurdle of getting them to follow up on the change in thought. While it is absolutely true that all of our behavior ultimately comes from our mind, our brains are still not simple masters of our actions. Rather, our actions are determined by multiple factors other than simply what our brain tells us to do. The reason you eventually have to ask your subject to change their actions directly is that, for new behaviors, a change in thought is just not enough.

Your subject needs voices other than the one in their head telling them what to do. They have the thought you got into their head through NLP; you are telling them directly, too. But there is still more you have to do.

Social bonds are incredibly important to human beings. If you want to manipulate someone's behavior, unlike when you persuade them into having new thoughts, these thoughts alone are not enough. You telling them what to do is not enough, even once they have recognized you as like them. If you want to change their behavior, next, you have to change the social environment of the person with the undesired behavior.

This is not a catch-all for manipulation, because nothing is. After all, not in every situation will you be able to change the social environment of your subject. If they are not friends or family, but rather a coworker, this could prove much more challenging. It is only fitting since manipulation is a more difficult and complicated task than persuasion.

But if this is a person whose social environment you have some control over, you have to determine what social factors are leading to undesired behaviors. Is there another family member enabling their drinking or drug use? This is the most prominent example, but all of it is emblematic of the NLP manipulation framework in general.

All of this is to say that when you are not in control of a person's social environment, directly telling them what action they should take is a necessary and challenging part of the process. It is so challenging because there is no way around it, and it is also very easy to do the wrong way.

You have to work hard not to work too hard for them. If they can see how badly you want them to change their behavior, they will want to continue acting the way they do out of spite. Don't give them this opportunity.

Recall how with persuasion we said never to address objections to your frame. In fact, if at all possible, you don't want to address the frame itself. That's because if you address the frame itself, you are acknowledging the fact that it is not the naturally occurring reality that you want your subject to see it as. However, with manipulation, the situation is different than it is for persuasion.

With manipulation, you have to respond to objections directly, because you have to tug harder than you do with persuasion. You see, persuasion is a subtler, quieter art than manipulation. This isn't a direct way of saying that manipulation is loud and aggressive, because it is not.

But you can't be quite as gentle with manipulation. You want them to change their habits, so in order to get your subject to understand the gravity of the situation enough to trigger the behavior change, it is necessary that you are slightly pushier than you are with persuasion. Again: don't be pushy, but you can't be as subtle as you are with persuasion.

Even when you deal with their objections, you are better off preparing for them before they come up. When you are ready for any question or complaint your subject can haul at you, it is a signal to them that you are like them, you see things from their side and perhaps you know better. This is Step One yet again. If you demonstrate that you are like them and can reason things out better, they will listen. You are almost ready to get into the techniques of manipulation, but before then, you need to get into the personality of the NLP manipulator.

You might think that you are born with a certain personality, and you can't do anything to change it, but this couldn't be further from the truth. In fact, the kind of personality you should adopt to get people to do what you want is one that anyone can learn.

Why is learning this personality so important? Well, it's important because you need to seem like you are positive about what you are saying. If you seem even a teensy bit unsure in any of your speech or your body language, nobody is going to buy what you are selling. That's why, in your body language, dress, facial expression, tone of voice and words, you need to pull off the personality of someone who knows what they are talking about.

They have the answer to your question; they know what's what. If you can pull off that personality, you basically don't have to do anything else. Personality is everything — don't forget that.

Personality is so important because no matter how unlikely something seems on the surface, if it comes out of the mouth of the right personality, people will believe in it. You have to believe in what you are saying to some extent if you expect to pull this off, so don't think you can play-act your way through the whole thing — after all, you are not doing the personality right if you are unsure about the merits of what you are saying. But more important than anything you say is the personality you are displaying while you say it.

Not everyone has this naturally, but it is not nearly as hard to learn as you might think. The right place to start is always your breathing and your posture. You already know what the right posture to take is — stand up straight and without shaking. Now, take deep breaths like for your state control exercises. Just like before, don't breathe loudly. Breathe deeply but not in a way that anyone can tell is unusual.

The third and final thing you have to do is enter the headspace of this unshakeable personality. Everyone has experienced a moment where everything was going right for them, and that is exactly the place you need to go. Revisit that memory as though you were there again right now and come back as the person you were in that memory.

The world is at your fingertips just like it was back then, especially if you carry this person inside of you. That person is necessary to succeed in manipulating people's behavior in the techniques coming up, so be sure you have your personality ready before reading. You won't be able to pull these off otherwise.

# Chapter 3:
## The Dark Triad

## THE DARK TRIAD

There are many ways to describe the cruel and inconsiderate among us. We can say they are mean, callous, awful, immoral, rude, depraved, unfeeling, heartless, and shady. We can talk endlessly about the qualities about the worst among us, but in the science of psychology, three qualities have emerged that best describe these sorts of people. We call these qualities "The Dark Triad." The dark triad consists of narcissism, psychopathy and Machiavellianism.

The dark triad is known to be the base of a lot of bad behavior, including lying, cheating, manipulation, impulsivity, and even murder and rape. It can be thought of as both a set of personality traits which can exist at varying levels in different individuals and also a device used by those high in these qualities to try to get away with mistreating others in all sorts of ways to satisfy themselves and get what they want easily and quickly.

The operative word here is quickly—while those whose personalities strongly exhibit personality components of the dark triad may get what they want oftentimes, their relationships are strained, destructive and fleeting. Naturally, those around them often catch on to their ways and, like a parasite, they need to find a new person or people to victimize. Now that we have some basic information, we can go into more depth about the three components—narcissism, psychopathy and Machiavellianism.

## Narcissism

At its most basic, narcissism describes a sense of extreme entitlement, lack of empathy, and excessive admiration of oneself. The word comes from the Greek myth of Narcissus, a young man who was so beautiful that he fell in love with his own reflection. He was callous and condescending towards those who loved him and drove some to commit suicide to prove their undying admiration for him. There are many signs an individual is narcissistic, and you have most likely met someone who displays this personality trait.

One of the most obvious signs of a narcissist is an excessive preoccupation with how they are perceived by others. They may spend an excessive amount of time grooming themselves and constantly presenting themselves in a light so positive that it treads on dishonest. The narcissist wants to be seen as a fabulous human being, constantly living it up and showing off their success and importance. They may exaggerate their achievements, social climb, or name drop about which important people they rub shoulders with.

In addition, the narcissist is an arrogant person who believes themselves to be more capable, important and worthy than those around them. They are often exploitative and lacking in empathy, which means that they will use others to get what they want, with no mind that it may be hurtful to the victim. Narcissists are able to do this because they view others as extensions of themselves and are unable to fathom that others have priorities that are dissimilar to their own—no favor is too big to ask for, and the narcissist's self-centeredness makes them believe that they are justified in their actions. The narcissist believes their needs are above those of others—why shouldn't others be extra considerate of them.

Think you've seen anger? Just wait until you meet narcissistic rage. Narcissistic rage is the outcome of a narcissistic injury. A narcissistic injury afflicts a narcissistic person when their grandiose opinion of themselves is challenged or shown to be faulty. For example, a narcissistic injury can come from being rejected by a potential romantic partner or getting turned down from a job. Having a response to rejection and disappointment this easily triggered is the result of a childhood trauma, such as a neglectful or abusive parent. The child, who senses that their parent does not love them, develops a grandiose persona in order to hide their deep feelings of inadequacy and shame and to convince themselves that they will be invulnerable to such suffering at the hands of another ever again. Essentially, a narcissist is constantly trying to cover up how insecure they really feel by pretending they are the greatest, most fabulous and accomplished human being of all time.

Once the injury occurs, the narcissist may fly into what is known as narcissistic rage. They will be unable to regulate their emotions and actions. The actions resulting from narcissistic rage can range anywhere from silent treatment and temporarily withdrawing from others all the way to physical violence and serious abuse. A narcissistic rage occurs because the narcissistic injury is simply too much to bear. To the narcissist, it calls into question how great they actually are and exposes them as imperfect beings.

There are many telltale signs of a narcissist and knowing some of their common behaviors can make them easier to spot. For one thing, they will take credit for good things that happen to them and blame bad outcomes on others, no matter what the reality of the situation is. If they get a bad grade on a project, they will insist that the professor has it out for them or that the grading process was unfair. If they have a good outcome, say someone of their preferred sex being friendly, they may insist this person was flirting with them. The narcissist wants to bend every story to present themselves in the most positive light and will not entertain any possibility that they may be wrong about something.

A narcissistic person is also obsessed with perfection. Not only do they hold themselves to high standards, which they often believe themselves to meet, but they also hold entities external to themselves to such a standard. The narcissist expects the people around them to behave perfectly, for events they attend to be perfect and their circumstances to be perfect. They will become irate if they feel others have not met their expectations, even if they are unreasonable.

Another sign you may be dealing with a narcissist is that they speak in extremes about those around them. For example, they may profess how "special" you are and how much they love you one day, but as soon as you irritate them, they will disparage, insult or neglect you. Despite a close relationship, a narcissist will always seem fairly uninterested in you as a person. You may tell them you had a bad day, or an interesting story about your day, and they will respond by talking about themselves. We have all had conversations like this—it's almost jarring. There you are, drinking coffee with a friend and believing both your and your friend's needs hold equal weight in the conversation, when they suggest otherwise by talking about themselves nonstop. They will ask you a few questions about yourself and if they do, but they seem to lose interest once you begin to reply. In short, what's the biggest sign someone is a narcissist? A narcissist will make you wonder if their life motto is "It's all about me!"

## Psychopathy

We often picture a psychopathic person to be a serial killer or a career criminal. In fiction, Patrick Bateman of American Psycho is seen as the quintessential psychopath — charming, brilliant, and unfathomably evil. Most psychopaths though will seem pretty normal to us. They are our co-workers sometimes, have been our classmates and maybe even our lovers and friends.

Psychopathy is referred to as Antisocial Personality Disorder (ASPD) in clinical settings. Psychopathy can exist along a spectrum; it is not an all or nothing quality. If someone were to take a personality test, they may score significantly higher than the population average on psychopathic tendencies but may still fall short of the necessary criteria for an ASPD diagnosis or may not exhibit antisocial behaviors sufficient for a diagnosis.

So, what characterizes psychopathy? First of all, psychopaths seem normal. They can be perfectly pleasant in conversations and give no hint about who they truly are. Underneath the normal exterior though, a psychopath is wicked. The psychopath lacks conscience, empathy and remorse. Because these qualities are absent, they are manipulative, self-serving and exploitative. Some even become criminals.

Another quality that defines psychopaths is a very high sensitivity to reward—when they want something, they want it badly, and they will do whatever is necessary to satisfy themselves. Many psychopaths are promiscuous and have many one-night stands. Being extra sensitive to reward combined with callousness and insensitivity means that psychopaths do not care about who gets hurt when they seek whatever appeals to them at the moment. Speaking of rewards, psychopaths will frequently use others to get what they want. They are keen on developing intimacy and trust, but once the main goal has been achieved, the psychopath discards the person they used, sometimes leaving a trail of emotional or financial devastation. Most psychopaths do not get treatment for ASPD. Not only do they believe there is nothing wrong with them, but their traits seem fairly fixed. Therapy and medication do not help change their thought patterns or often sadistic methods of controlling others. Consider yourself lucky if you have not been affected by a psychopath. They often wreak havoc on the lives of those they get close to.

In general, psychopaths will often seem to lack emotion. If a tragedy occurs, they may seem impossibly unaffected. They are also practically fearless compared to the rest of us—they are afraid of neither getting hurt nor getting caught. Overall, their emotions are shallow. They may enjoy someone's company, but they don't really care about this person. The psychopath often lives for pleasure and power — human connection and emotion mean little to them.

Like narcissists, psychopaths also have a hard time accepting responsibility. Because of this and their lack of fear, they are often reckless and irresponsible. Not only do they behave irresponsibly, they also insist that whatever they have caused is not their fault. Eventually, even if a psychopath is forced to accept blame, they will seem not to care. They do not see their irresponsible ways as an indictment of their skills, character or ability. They see no reason to change because it's always someone else's fault.

Last but not least in the most important traits to look out for are the psychopath's intense selfishness and egocentricity. The psychopath often lives a parasitic lifestyle, which is to say they use others to meet their own needs without thought about how this may affect the victim being bled dry. What does this look like? A psychopath may get close to you and then constantly ask you for money, whether or not they have enough of their own. If you are married to a psychopath, you are probably the one who constantly cleans the house and cooks dinner unless your psychopathic spouse sees incentive to complete those tasks. Often, this is how psychopaths destroy lives. They may have children with a partner who feeds and cares for them and abandon this family eventually. They often take and take and take until their partner is completely broke and financially destitute. This is the parasitic lifestyle at play — the psychopath will suck your blood without you even noticing until you have none left. Once there is nothing for the parasite to take, they cut and run because you have nothing left to give them. It is estimated that up to twenty-five percent of incarcerated individuals suffer from ASPD.

## Machiavellianism

Before we get into Machiavellianism, let us understand the word's namesake, Niccolò Machiavelli. Niccolò Machiavelli was an Italian statesman during the Italian renaissance in the fifteenth and sixteenth centuries. He was a diplomat, politician, secretary, philosopher, poet, historian, humanist and playwright. He is known today for his book "Il Principe" or "The Prince." The book is a deep analysis into the acquisition and maintenance of political power, written so Machiavelli could return to Italian politics from exile and hopefully be appointed a political advisory position by the Medici family. The book was so shocking at the time that Machiavelli was labeled an atheist. Machiavelli advocated for ruthless, cunning, and strategic methods of gaining and keeping political power. He is often credited with the saying, "the ends justify the means."

Given this introduction of Machiavelli the man, a deeper discussion of Machiavellianism as a member of the dark triad is appropriate. Machiavellianism includes low empathy, prioritizing power over others, strong ambition, and exploitation of others for personal gain. Machiavellianism is different from psychopathy because of the Machiavellian's emphasis on exploitation for personal gain, whereas a psychopath's very nature is insensitivity and callousness no matter what.

The Machiavellian believes human nature is inherently evil, and that deception is a justifiable way to attain goals and success. They generally undervalue human connection and overvalue wealth and power. They believe depending on others and cultivating meaningful emotional relationships is a worthless endeavor. When they manipulate or exploit others, they believe they have acted with reason and can justify their actions. They will do something terrible to complete a goal and when confronted, they will say, "Hey, I got the job done, right? It all worked out."

So, how do you know you're dealing with a Machiavellian? The Machiavellian is notoriously low on empathy; human connection always comes second to achievement and personal gain. To a Machiavellian, people are often conduits to other things — money, power, sex, or whatever else may seem worthwhile to achieve. Machiavellians are known to lie and exploit when necessary in order to get what they want.

Another common quality of Machiavellians is their penchant for strategy and calculation. A Machiavellian is good at sizing up others. They can read the room so to speak and are perceptive of others' thoughts, feelings and weaknesses, despite the low empathy that accompanies Machiavellianism. Due to this calculating nature, these people tend to be patient. They are constantly collecting information and analyzing it to use to their best advantage. They know how to plan and wait for their rewards.

The demeanor of a Machiavellian often falls into one of two camps. They either seem aloof and emotionally distant or charming and friendly. Note that both of these demeanors may be present in the same person; someone may be charming and friendly, but reveal so little about themselves that you may become suspicious or realize well into a relationship of any kind with the Machiavellian that you know little about them. This is deliberate, as the Machiavellian generally prefers not to share their true intentions with others.

With respect to their morals, Machiavellians are unlike psychopaths. While the psychopath simply lacks morals, the Machiavellian is scattered, inconsistent and ill-defined. The Machiavellian may claim to have certain ethical principles they value highly, but they are certainly willing to ignore them if they can justify doing so. Generally speaking, they have little respect for humanity as a whole. They think it is inherently evil, or at the very least not good, and are usually cynical.

## How to Spot These PEOPLE?

The dark triad can take shape in numerous ways. Generally, the actions that result from these qualities can have a seriously damaging effect on others. All traits of the dark triad have one important thing in common—they lead the narcissist, psychopath, or Machiavellian to believe other people do not matter as much as themselves. Because they believe this (consciously or unconsciously), they consistently place their own needs above the needs of others, often being hurtful, harmful and inconsiderate in the process.

When it comes to the specifics of how a Machiavellian behaves, you have probably encountered a Machiavellian leader before. They may be a politician, a boss or a high school mean girl. Your Machiavellian leader probably attempted to inspire fear and respect among subordinates. They wanted admiration but not as much as they lusted for loyalty and fear-induced deference from others. They were also probably ruthless in their quest for power; perhaps their ascent required the humiliation or betrayal of someone. Maybe your boss used some dirty tricks to get their job, or the high school mean girl spread a vicious rumor about a social rival to eliminate her as a threat or competitor for social capital.

Psychopaths, while similarly lacking in empathy, tend to be a bit more pleasure-driven than Machiavellians and may be a little bit less calculating. Psychopaths are not reliable or predictable per se, but most engage in some pretty typical behavior for their personality.

They tend to be promiscuous and enjoy casual sexual encounters. They are not above lying or using sneaky seduction tactics, including dishonesty, in order to achieve this. More importantly, those who commit violent crimes, regardless of whether they are sadistic, are more likely to be psychopaths. Why? Because psychopaths lack empathy and are incapable of caring that they may hurt another human being. In addition, they have low impulse control. If a psychopath gets angry enough, they may harm another human being simply because their rage drives them to do so, and they have no empathy serving to slow them down and reconsider the consequences of their actions. Psychopaths are generally as manipulative as narcissists. They will engage in many CEM tactics like guilt tripping and gaslighting to get what they want.

## Sadism

Sadism is a trait common among those who are high in narcissism, psychopathy and/or Machiavellianism. Sadism is the tendency to find enjoyment in causing pain to other living beings, human or otherwise. While sadism is commonly associated with sexual pleasure derived from inflicting pain on another human being, it can certainly be non-sexual.

Sadistic individuals are low on empathy, which is why they would not have the same internal cringe as a non-sadist when they inflict pain. They are unable to feel the secondhand pain they cause to their victim, so they do not get the twisted, nauseous feeling most of us would experience if we were to hurt an innocent person.

Usually, when we imagine a sadist, they are a murderer slowly torturing their victim before finishing them off. This is not the case in everyday life though. Plenty of sadistic individuals do not need to go to such extremes to satisfy their urges. Sadists get off on the power they have over someone else by hurting them. This is why a sadist may seem like they enjoy humiliating others in person. They want to watch their victim suffer.

For example, a sadist may also create problems at work or in their social circle to watch the rest of the group gang up on someone. Here, the sadist enjoys the difficulty and pain they cause to the individual, while also creating unrest and chaos in the group. They like that they can stir up so much pain. They also make mean "jokes" at someone's expense. They like making jokes about their friends', family's, or partner's biggest insecurity to watch their confidence be undermined. Once again, they live to see people feel small and helpless so they can feel powerful themselves.

At their most extreme, sadists can be violent and cruel. They often have a high threshold for disgust, so watching pain does not disturb them. The most extreme sadists tend to be those high in psychopathy. These people are the ones often covered in the news for heinous, bloody crimes—the serial killers who started off torturing and killing small animals when they were children.

The three traits of the dark triad covered in this chapter— narcissism, psychopathy, and Machiavellianism—represent the worst humanity has to offer. They are the three prongs of a nasty pitchfork of hostility and antisocial behavior. Beware of those you believe to match the descriptions of these personality types, if possible. As the biggest takers and cheaters in the world, they have serious potential to create damage and pain in your life. If you cannot avoid contact with them, at least attempt not to cross their bad side. This does not mean completely foregoing your own needs to placate them, but try not to argue with them too much and avoid them when possible. Once again, get out of these relationships as quickly as possible or minimize your contact and dependence on them.

## COMMON TRAITS

### <u>Use of Language</u>

We have shown how powerful language can be, as a prime tool of persuasion. There is more to the manipulative controller though than mere words. They will use tactics that mislead and unbalance their target's inner thoughts. We now understand that through language, they will:

- Use mistruths to mislead and confuse their target's normal thinking pattern.

- Force their target to make a decision at speed, so they don't have time to analyze and think.

- Talk to their target in an overwhelming manner, making them feel small.

- Criticize their target's judgment so they begin to lose their own self-esteem.

- Raise the tone of their voice and not be afraid to use aggressive body language.

- Ignore their target's needs; they are only interested in getting what they want and at any cost.

## Invasion of Personal Space

Most of us set boundaries around ourselves without realizing we are doing so. It is a kind of unspoken rule to protect our own private space, such as not sitting so close that you are touching another person, especially a stranger. A manipulative character cares nothing about overstepping such boundaries. Whether this is because they do not understand, or they do not care is unclear. Initially, they are unlikely to invade their target's personal space. They will seek to build up a good rapport first. This shows that they do understand boundaries because once they gain the confidence of their target, they will then ignore them.

## Fodder for Thought

Manipulators tend to be very ego-centric, with limited social skills. Their only concern is for themselves. Everything they do in life will be in relation to how it affects them, not how their actions affect others. Does this mean that they have a psychopathic disorder?

They lack sympathy of any kind because another's weakness is simply a tool for them. When they detect any weakness in their target's resolve or personality, they will exploit it. The consequences to their victim are of little importance. The target's weaknesses feed the manipulator's strength, making them bolder and often crueler in their actions.

## **Creating Rivalry**

Another tactic of the controlling manipulator is backstabbing. They may tell you how great a person you are to your face, making them look good. Behind your back, they are busy spreading malicious gossip and untruths about you. This is a classic trait of a controlling manipulator as it creates a rivalry between people. Then, they can pick a side that will make them look favorable, particularly to their target. It can act as the first stage to getting close to their target.

## **Domineering Personality**

It is unlikely that a manipulative person will outwardly show any form of weakness. An important part of their facade is to show conviction about their views. They seek to impress, believing they are right about everything, almost to the point that, if they realize they are wrong, they will still argue that they are right. On a one-to-one level, that invariably means that your position is always wrong. As they chip away at your beliefs, they seek to undermine your sense of self-esteem. Once they have achieved this, there is no holding them back. They seek to domineer over others, often speaking with a condescending tone to belittle their victims. Using ridicule is yet another tool against their target, merely because it will make them look better. If you ridicule them back, they will seek to turn the tables, accusing you of being oversensitive to their "joke." It's the kind of joke where only the teller sees the funny side.

## Passive Aggressive Behavior

A common trait of many hard-core manipulators is passive aggressive behavior. Because they prefer to be popular, they do not wish to be seen as doing anything wrong. Not that a manipulator would ever admit to doing anything wrong. They are experts with facial expressions that are meant to dominate and intimidate. This may include; knitting eyebrows, grinding teeth and rolling eyes. It may also include noises such as tutting and grunting sounds. It is very common behavior for such a character, as there is little anyone else has to say that they will agree with. For most manipulators, it is their life's ambition to show people up by proving them wrong.

## Moody Blues

What of the emotional stability of the manipulator? Is it that which makes them behave the way they do? Do they even know what happiness is? The answer to that is a most definite yes, at least to the latter.

Happiness is a tool used initially to help them manipulate, a happy target is more likely to comply. This in itself makes the manipulator happy, at least in a sense of what they consider happiness. But their joyfulness is a perverted model of what most others consider happiness to be. Their happiness is often built on the foundations of another's misery - misery that they have caused with their cruel manipulations. Equally though, a manipulator is prone to mood swings. These are most likely to happen when things are not going to plan. One minute they are euphoric at their latest conquest; the next they could be completely deflated at their failure to succeed. One thing is certain for those who live with or become a target of this type of domineering character - they will be unhappy all the time.

## Intimidation

One aspect of manipulation, often used as a last resort, is intimidation and bullying. When everything else has failed, they begin to use threats to get their own way. Some though may use intimidation from the onset. It may be a source of authority. For example, let's take the role of a manipulative boss. You have requested a day off. They don't want to allow you your request, but have no choice, it is your right. This type of person would want their pound of flesh first. They will set goals for you to reach so it will delay or cancel your request, such as moving project deadlines forward. This way they have their little victory over you.

# Chapter 5:
# Mind Control And Mind Games

## WHAT IS MIND CONTROL?

The concept of mind control has existed for as long as psychology has been studied. You have probably overheard a person express their fascination or fear concerning what would happen if there was ever a chance that someone was able to control the minds of others and make them follow their commands. Similarly, there have been multiple conspiracy theories running around about powerful people or authorities utilizing their positions to force small groups of people to do certain things. There have even been court cases where the accused people blame "brainwashing" for causing them to commit their crimes. Collectively, these three examples tell us that people understand that mind control is real.

However, the form of mind control that people seem to define is that which has been portrayed by the movies and media, which, unfortunately, is just but the tip of the iceberg. Mind control exists in many forms, and people appear to understand very little about it. This pushes the need for a definite understanding and description of what exactly mind control is. If we take the words of psychologist Philip Zimbardo, mind control is defined as a process whereby the freedom of action and choice of an individual or a group is compromised by agencies or agents that distort or modify motivation, perception, behavioral and/or cognitive outcomes. In summary, mind control is a system that disrupts a person or group at their core, that is, the level of their identity (which includes behaviors, decisions, preferences, beliefs, and relationships, to mention but a few) and creates a pseudo personality or pseudo-identity.

The above descriptions make it clear a person might be wrong to assume that they are forever in charge of their actions and thoughts. By now, you should already know that our minds are not solely at our discretion since they are susceptible to influence and control. Let us take a very common example. When you are watching an emotional movie, the directors utilize camera shots, lighting, color, music and other enhancements to control your emotions. In as much as you are aware that what you are watching is not real, your brain still plays along, and you find yourself engrossed in the movie. Some people weep at sad scenes, whereas others jump or cringe when watching horror movies.

Now, think about it; if your brain can respond to a prompt which it clearly understands is not real, how would it react to hidden (covert) prompts? This brings us to covert mind control, which is the form of mind control where the victim is not aware that any distortion is being applied. Covert mind control is the most brutal form of control known to psychologists today. This is because if a person realizes that they are being controlled, they can try to escape the situation, unlike in covert mind control where one never gets to know it. The result is the controller takes full charge and might drive the victim to destruction without them realizing it.

Mind control can be ethical or unethical. You might wonder how having your mind shaped by another person can be good for you. Well, a good example of ethical mind control began when you were growing up. When your parents were bringing you up, they applied a lot of mind control. You are the person that you are today because of this mind control. Most of the beliefs, values and behaviors that you possess, though you might have altered some, were passed onto you by your parents. Let's get a little more practical: when you wake up, your immediate actions include brushing your teeth, taking a shower, jumping into fresh clothes, applying makeup and having breakfast before anything else. Where do you think this routine came from? It was passed onto you by your parents or guardians.

Let us now look at the mind control process in detail.

## Understanding the target

Before anything else, the manipulator will seek to establish a bond or connection with their potential victim. Good intent, or friendship, will be the first step because it makes the victim lower all their social and psychological defenses. Once the controller gains the trust of the target, they now start reading them to devise the most effective method to invade them. The reading aims to tell whether their victim is susceptible to their manipulation. Just like any project manager, they do not like wasting time on a subject they suspect might outsmart them and lead to failure.

Multiple clues are used to scan the victim. They include verbal style, body language, social status, gender, emotional stability and so on. A person's traits can be used to decode the strength of their defenses. All this time, the manipulator will be asking themselves questions like, "Are you an introvert or extrovert?" "Are you weakly?" "Are you emotional?" "Are you self-confident?" Humans give a lot of information about themselves when interacting with each other, and this is something that the controller knows all too well. From these signs, they can easily tell if the person is cooperating. They will look at body posture and immediately analyze the victim. Excessive blinking might insinuate that a person is lying. Arms folded across the chest might show a lack of interest or insecurity. Taking large strides while walking might portray fear. As you can see, the body releases so much data at any given time that it is important to be aware of the signs that you are giving out (this will be covered in detail later in this book).

When the attacker has collected enough data from the target, they now understand their interests, strengths, weaknesses, routines and so on. Using this information, they can decide on an entry point which will allow for easy and accurate manipulation. They also decide whether the target is worth the effort. If they see one as a favorable target, they move to the next step in the mind control process - unfreezing solid beliefs and values.

## Unfreezing Solid Beliefs and Values

Each one of us has some beliefs and values engraved deep within. Most of them are the principles that were instilled in us since childhood, and others have been acquired from experiences as we grow older. We rarely let go of them but revise them as we proceed. Most of them are what make up our identities, so we do not like them being interfered with. If at any point in time, these principles are threatened, contradicted or questioned, our natural reaction is to defend them through all means possible. However, if a good-enough reason is given to us, we voluntarily question them ourselves; we undergo a process known as "unfreezing."

Tons of reasons can lead us to unfreeze: a breakup, the death of a loved one, religious interference, getting evicted from our houses, to mention but a few. These situations force us to start seeking answers to complex situations, and this goes as deep as questioning our sole beliefs and values. Take this, for example:

When I was a teenager, we had some family friends who were solid Christians. It so happened that my best friend, who was my exact age, came from this family. His name was Sam. Sam used to tell me about the Bible and its teachings, trying to convince me to accept salvation and live according to its teachings. I remember asking him why he was so insistent on this issue, and he would respond that with salvation, all problems were solvable and that life was much easier and happier. Fast-forward about fifteen years, Sam's mother was diagnosed with breast cancer. They tried all forms of treatment available at the time, but cancer would grow back. One day, while talking to him about the issue, he looked at me with a pale face and said, "I think what they say about Christianity is not real!" Unsure about what he had just said, I asked him why he thought so. He responded that they had met tens of spiritual leaders for prayers, but his mother's cancer was only getting worse. What's worse; she would not live for more than a year.

Sad as Sam's story is, it makes us realize that some situations in life might force us to question the strong principles that we grow up with. In this case, my best friend had come to doubt the very same religion that he once felt had automatic solutions to all of life's problems. In the very same manner, a manipulator will dig deep into their victim's life to understand their vulnerabilities and exploit them fully. These people will say anything they think their targets would love to hear. Once the victim swallows the manipulator's comfort, there is a shift in power dynamics, and the target is now ready for the manipulation.

## Reprogramming the Mind

The mind control process seeks to separate the target from their initial beliefs and begin reprogramming their mind. The reprogramming is meant to install the manipulator's beliefs and values into the victim's mind. Apart from distancing the initial principles, the controller also tries their best to make them look wrong, bad or the cause of past mishaps in the victim's life. If the victim absorbs this reprogramming, their defense is lowered to zero, and they now become a robot that is ready to accept any operating system that is offered.

During the reprogramming phase, the attacker will try to ensure the victim has minimal contact with the outside world. They make everyone else appear insignificant to the victim because this raises their opportunity to deposit their malicious principles into them. This behavior is common in cults, which are mostly crafted to sway their followers from mainstream human life. Some cults go as far as controlling the food intake of their followers as a way of weakening them. The psychology behind this idea is that a weak person will always turn to the person they feel has the power to protect them or alleviate their suffering. The same happens in relationships, where one partner plays the controlling role, and the victimized one has no choice but to adhere to the other. You might wonder why some people put up with violent partners, but so far, from reading this book, you must already understand that the problem is deeper than it appears. If you control a person's mind, you can control their lives.

Once the victim has been reprogrammed, the manipulator moves into the final phase of the mind control process known as "freezing."

## Freezing the New Beliefs and Values

Do you remember the "unfreezing" process we discussed earlier? So, once the victim has been fed with contrasting principles by the offender, the offender applies tactics aimed at cementing the new beliefs into their brains. This is what psychologists call "freezing." The freezing bit is necessary because the controller is aware of the person's new beliefs that might clash with their initial ones. As such, they need to force the victim to choose their malicious principles over their old ones. To do this, they might apply any of the following methods.

One of the methods is using the reward/punishment approach. When the victim acts according to the manipulator's demands, they are rewarded. Hopefully, you see the similarity between the freezing process and dog training. The dog is given treats when it follows the trainer's instructions. The trainer aims at solidifying the new skill in the dog by rewarding it. In the future, if the dog is instructed to do the same thing, it will not hesitate since it has been made to think that obeying the command is good and attracts a reward. The same applies to mind control; when the victim obeys, they are made to feel that what they did was right and deserves a reward.

Punishments are the second most-applied approach in the freezing process. If the victim deviates from the controller's commands, they are punished. If we go back to the scenario of a cult, they usually have defined punishments for violations of terms. During the Holocaust, for instance, any Germans who failed to hail Hitler were punished through imprisonment or death. In the same way, any German who was suspected of protecting the Jews was shot. Hitler understood that by punishing anyone who went against his rules, he would force every German to help him attain his objective of ethnic cleansing. The psychological trick used in these situations is that the victim is made to see punishment as justice being served for breaking the rules.

The final method used by mind controllers to solidify their manipulation is to transform their victims into their agents. Better put, once the controller feels that the victim's pseudo personality has materialized, they use them to distribute their worldviews. At the beginning of this book, we said that the agenda of the mind controller is to create a replica of themselves in the other person. Therefore, once the controlling process is complete, the victim starts living like the attacker without realizing it. Depending on the nature of the manipulation, the victim might also be used to recruit more victims into the oppressor's way of thinking and living. This is especially true in the context of marketing and networking, which we shall discuss under the topic of deception. From this explanation, we can readily tell why a wife is likely to be violent towards the kids if the husband is violent. The kids are also likely to be violent towards each other or their friends. The process of mind control is slow, but once it solidifies, it can result in devastating effects.

## MIND CONTROL TECHNIQUES

Mind control involves using influence and persuasion to change the behaviors and beliefs in someone. That someone might be the person themselves or it might be someone else. Mind control has also been referred to as brainwashing, thought reform, coercive persuasion, mental control, and manipulation, just to name a few. Some people feel that everything is done by manipulation. But if that is to be believed, then important points about manipulation will be lost. Influence is much better thought of as a mental continuum with two extremes. One side has influences that are respectful and ethical and work to improve the individual while showing respect for them and their basic human rights. The other side contains influences that are dark and destructive that work to remove basic human rights from a person, such as independence, the ability for rational thought and sometimes their total identity.

When thinking of mind control, it is better to see it as a way to use influence on other people that will disrupt something in them, like their way of thinking or living. Influence works on the very basis of what makes people human, such as their behaviors, beliefs and values. It can disrupt the very way they choose personal preferences or make critical decisions. Mind control is nothing more than using words and ideas to convince someone to say or do something they might never have thought of saying or doing on their own.

There are scientifically proven methods that can be used to influence other people. Mind control has nothing to do with fakery, ancient arts or even magical powers. Real mind control really is the basis of a word that many people hate to hear. That word is marketing. Many people hate to hear that word because of the negative connotations associated with it. When people hear "marketing," they automatically assume that it refers to those ideas taught in business school. But the basis of marketing is not about deciding which part of the market to target or deciding which customers will likely buy this product. The basis of marketing is one very simple word. That word is "YES."

If a salesperson asks a regular customer to write a brief endorsement of the product they buy, hopefully they will say yes. If someone asks their significant other to take some of the business cards to pass out at work, hopefully they will say yes. If you write any kind of blog and ask another blogger to provide a link to yours on their blog, hopefully they will say yes. When enough people say yes, the business or blog will begin to grow. With even more yeses, it will continue to grow and thrive. This is the very simple basis of marketing. Marketing is nothing more than using mind control to get other people to buy something or to do something beneficial for someone else. And the techniques can easily be learned.

The first technique in mind control is to tell people what you want them to want. Never tell people to think it over or take some time. That is a definite mind control killer. People already have too much going on in their minds. When they are told to think something over they will not. It will be forgotten, and then it will never happen. This has nothing to do with being stupid or lazy and everything to do with just being way too busy.

So the best strategy is to take the offensive and think for them. Everything must be explained in the beginning. Never assume that the other blogger will automatically understand the benefits of adding a link will be for them. Do not expect anyone to give a demonstration blindly. And merely asking for a testimonial, while it might garner an appositive response, probably will not garner a well-formed testimonial to the product. Instead, be prepared to explain the blog, show examples, and offer compelling reasons why this merger will be a benefit to both parties. Have the demonstration laid out in great detail with notes on what to say when and visuals to go along with the notes, so all the other person has to do is present the information. Offer the customer a few variations of testimonials that have already been received and ask them to choose one and personalize it a bit. Always be specific in explaining what is desired. Explain why it is desired. Show how this will work. Tell the person how to do it and why they should do it. If done correctly, it will feel exactly like one friend advising another friend on which is the best path to take. And the answer will be yes simply because saying yes makes so much sense.

Think of the avalanche. Think of climbing all the way to the top of the highest mountain ever. Now, at the top, think of searching for the biggest heaviest boulder that exists on the mountain. Now, picture summoning up superhuman strength to push this boulder, dislodging it from the place it has rested for years and years. Once this boulder is loosened, it rolls easily over the edge of the cliff, crashing into thousands of other boulders on its way down the mountain, taking half of the mountain with it in a beautiful cascade of rocks and dirt. Imagine sitting there smiling cheerfully at the avalanche that was just created.

Marketing and mind control are very like creating an avalanche. Getting the first person to answer yes might be difficult. But each subsequent yes will be easier and easier. And always start at the top, never the bottom. Starting at the top is definitely more difficult, and it is more likely to come with more negative responses than positive responses in the beginning. But starting at the top also yields a much greater reward when the avalanche does begin. And the results will be far greater than beginning at the bottom of the mountain. Yes, the small rock is easier to push over. Then it can be built upon by pushing over another small rock, then another. This way can work, but it will take much longer than being successful at the top. No one ever went fishing for the smallest fish in the pond or auditioned for the secondary role just to be safe. Everyone wants that top prize. Do not be afraid to go for it.

On the other hand, never ask for the whole boulder the first time. Ask for part of it. This may seem directly contradictory but it is not. Always start with a small piece. Make the beginning easier for everyone to see. Let other people use their own insight to see the end result. When the first bit goes well, then gradually ask for more and more and more.

Think of writing a guest spot for someone else who has their own blog. By sending in the entire manuscript first, there is a greater risk of rejection. Begin small. Send them a paragraph or two discussing the idea. Then make an outline of the idea and send that in an email. Then write the complete draft you would like them to use and send it along. When asking a customer for a testimonial, start by asking for a few lines in an email. Then ask the customer to expand those few lines into a testimonial that covers at least half a typed page. Soon the customer will be ready for an hour-long webcast extolling the virtues of the product and your great customer service skills.

Everything must have a deadline that really exists. The important word here is the word 'real'. Everyone has heard the salesperson who said to decide quickly because the deal might not be available later or another customer was coming in and they might get it. That is a total fabrication and everyone knows it to be true. There are no impending other customers and the deal is not going to disappear. There is no real sense of urgency involved. But everyone does it. There are too many situations where people are given a totally fake deadline by someone who thinks it will instill a great sense of urgency for completion of the task. It is not only completely ineffective, but completely unneeded. It is a simple matter of creating true urgency. Only leave free things available for a finite amount of time. When asking customers for testimonials, be certain to mention the last possible day for it to be received to be able to be used. Some people will be unable to assist, but having people unable to participate is better than never being able to begin.

Always give before you receive. And do not ever think that giving is fifty-fifty. Always give much more than is expected in return. Before asking for a testimonial from a satisfied customer, be sure to make numerous acts of exceptional customer service. Before asking a blog writer for a link, link theirs to yours many times. This is not about helping someone out so they will help you. This is all about being so totally generous that the person who is asked for the favor cannot possibly say no. It might mean extra work, but that is how to influence other people.

Always stand up for something that is much bigger than average. Do not just write another blog on how to do something. Use an important issue to take a stand and defend the stance with unbeatable logic and fervent passion. Do not just write a how-to manual. Choose a particular idea and sell people on it, using examples of other people with the same idea living the philosophy.

Never feel shame. This does not mean being extremely extroverted to the point of silliness or having a total lack of conscience in business dealings. In the case of mind control, shamelessness refers to a complete belief that this course of action is the best possible course and everyone will benefit greatly from it. This is about writing the best possible blog ever and believing that everyone needs to read it to be able to improve their lives. It is about believing in a particular product so deeply that the feeling is that everyone will benefit from using it. It is knowing deep inside that this belief is the most correct belief ever and everyone should believe it.

Mind control uses the idea that someone's decisions and emotions can be controlled using psychological means. It is using powers of negotiation or mental influence to ensure the outcome of the interaction is more favorable to one person over the other. This is basically what marketing is: convincing someone to do something particular or buy something in particular. Being able to control someone else's mind merely means understanding the power of human emotion and being able to play upon those emotions. It is easier to have a mental impact on people if there is a basic understanding of human emotions. Angry people will back down when the subject of their anger is not afraid. Angry people feed upon the fear of others. Guilt is another great motivator. Making someone feel guilty for not thinking or feeling in the same manner is a wonderful way to get them to give in. Another way to use mind control over someone is to point out how valuable they are to the situation.

## MIND GAMES

When a person plays "mind games" on us, it is attributed to being innocent. Many people have come across this at some point in their lives. Take an example when someone is planning a surprise party, doesn't want the other person to know and does this by playing mind tricks in order not to give away what the surprise actually is. This is merely considered innocent and silly. Dark psychology mind games are not in any way innocent. Mind games in dark psychology are attributed to the hypnotist toying with the will power and sanity of his victim. This differs from other dark psychological manipulation in the sense that the manipulator is playing with his victim for their own pleasure and enjoyment and is not invested in what the outcome will be. Their interest in the victim would be to test the them, so to speak. Mind games are used by a hypnotist when other forms of suggestions to the victim are not effective and may decide to use mind games which are rather less obvious to the audience. The manipulator may decide to use mind games for their own pleasure and amusement. Mind games are very effective in reducing the assuredness and psychological strength of the victim. The victim is deluded into thinking that the manipulator still has control. Manipulators are able to satisfy their twisted amusement when playing mind games. Such dark psychological manipulators do not see their victims as equal human beings and instead choose to see the victim as a 'toy' and a person who can be manipulated and therefore watch with amusement when victims do what they tell them to. Sometimes, a dark manipulator will have known mind games all their life and knows no other forms of dark psychology manipulation. These manipulators can be dangerous because they know not of any other option and therefore feel no need to change and be more humane. Let us dive into the specific types of mind games used by dark manipulators.

You have heard of mind games. You have surely played them before and had them played on you. You can use mind games as an effective persuasion tool when you know what to do and when. There are numerous techniques that are effective, and they are not that difficult to learn. This means that once you know what they are, you can start utilizing mind games right away to start getting what you want. Here are some of mind games techniques:

## Kick Me

This likely reminds you of that game when you were a kid where you put a sign on someone's back that read "kick me." This is similar. You want to make yourself look like someone that deserves pity. Once you get pity from someone, it is easier to get them to do what you want. You can use this for just about anything in life from getting someone to allow you to apologize to getting a boss to give you a promotion once you get really good at it.

## Now That I've Got You

This is a game that you will use when you want to show a person you are winning and better. You can also use it when you are angry and want to justify it. For example, your friend had a party, but he neglected to invite you. So, you decide to host a party the following weekend with the intent to just not invite him. This game basically has you working to one up another person to get them to give in and give you what you want.

## You Made Me Do It

This is another one you used during childhood and you likely did not even realize at the time that it was a type of mind game. This is a game that works to make another person feel guilty while simultaneously absolving you of any responsibility for your actions. For example, you want to be left alone. However, someone comes in the room to ask you a question. As a result, you are startled and drop your beverage. You tell that person that they made you drop your beverage.

## If It Weren't for You

This is another mind game that is used to absolve yourself of any guilt for something you might have done. With this type of game, you essentially create a scenario that allows you to put guilt onto someone. This gives you an array of advantages. When a person is feeling guilty about something, they are more vulnerable to suggestion. For example, you are unable to go to work for whatever reason. You find a way to blame your spouse for this and make them feel guilty. As a result, you are able to coerce your spouse into making you a meal or buying you something.

## Let You Both Fight

The purpose of this mind game is to share blame, control other people and even make yourself seem like a good friend. In most cases, this is a mind game that women will play, but it is becoming more common among men. For example, a person knows that two people are attracted to them. This person then talks both of the interested parties into fighting with one another to basically win their heart. This is basically a type of transaction; however, at the end of the game, both interested parties are usually left without anyone.

## RAPO

This mind game can be a major ego boost, give a sense of satisfaction and increase how desirable you see yourself to be. It is a type of social game in which you essentially convince a person to pursue you. You convince them in a way that is not obvious to them, so they do not even know what it is happening. How you choose to convince them is flexible and really dependent on your preferences and what it takes to get into the subconscious of the person you are seeking to lure. What is good about this game is that it generally does not take long to put into practice.

## Perversion

The purpose of this game is to avoid responsibility and garner sympathy. Basically, this mind game is used to seduce another person. You cause them to feel guilty if they are not fulfilling your romantic needs. You talk about a bad past relationship, whether it was real or not, to first get sympathy from them. Then, once they essentially soften to the idea of fulfilling your desires, you go in and take what you want. If they are still resistant, you cause them to feel guilty to ultimately get what you want.

## Clever Me

This one improves your identity, social capital, attention and ego. You do something to show someone what you are great at and you want the entire world to know that you are awesome at this specific thing. You manipulate the situation to make sure that someone will learn about your skill. You get attention from them and they tell others. Before you know it, your skill or talent is being spread around and a lot of people are coming to you to pay you a compliment.

## Wooden Leg

This is a game people play for sympathy, as a plea of insanity or to avoid responsibility. You have likely heard the saying that you can only expect so much from a person who has a wooden leg. This game is built upon this saying. Basically, you use a perceived shortfall or disability to gain sympathy and make your actions seem justified. For example, you just cheated on your spouse and they found out. You would say something like, "Well, my parents had a bad marriage, so what do you expect of me?" They then start to give you sympathy and you are absolved of your guilt.

## The Double Request

This is a common mind game among those who want something big but know that they will not get it by just asking. For example, you ask for a new expensive watch, but you really want a new jacket that tends to be less expensive. You mention both items, but you make it seem like the watch is what you truly desire. In the end, the friend you are talking to remembers that the jacket was cheaper and also something that you wanted, so they buy it. You end up getting the jacket you wanted from the start.

## You're a Good Person

This is a common mind game to play when you want to get something out of someone that they are not normally asked. When you start the conversation by telling them that they are a good person, they are getting recognition and an ego boost from you.

This already softens them and makes them more prone to give you exactly what you want. Once you see that their body language is softer or even just neutral, you want to go in and ask for what you want.

# Chapter 6:
## Profile of a Manipulator In Detail

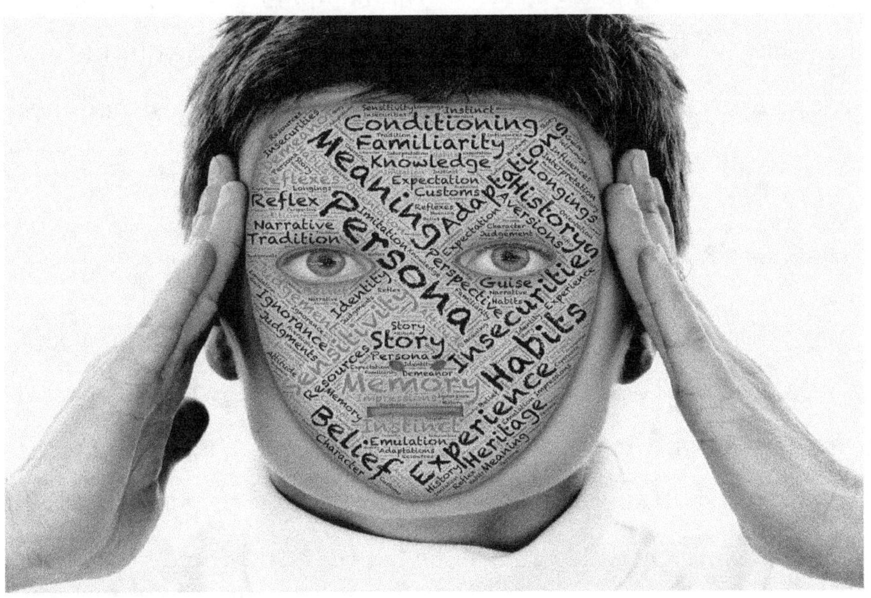

## DEFEATING MANIPULATION

It is one thing to understand manipulation, and how it works and can wreak havoc on your life. Understanding all the different tricks and tactics that a manipulator can use against you may make it seem like it is impossible to defend yourself against manipulation. But the truth is that, by understanding in excellent detail how manipulators can use a wide array of tactics against you, you use their weapons against them, something they are not expecting.

To understand a potential enemy and the tactics they might use is to beat them at their own game. Too often manipulators enter our lives because we find their companionship pleasing, so we let them fill a need that they create. This need can come from many places, for some a broken home, for others a simple need for action. To not know yourself is the greatest asset a manipulator can use against you. They act like parasites burrowing their way into your life and sucking you dry, getting all that they can resource-wise and then leaving you.

## YOU CAN PROTECT YOURSELF

The good news is that you can avoid having this happen to you if you don't let it. Too often we let people dictate how they can treat us by our actions. If we let someone convince us that we are weak and need them to succeed then is it their fault for us getting sucked into their web. Or is it perhaps our fault for convincing ourselves that this "relationship" is good for us? The truth of the matter is that manipulators like to prey on people who have been hurt before. Their charm and glib cons us into thinking that they will help us with whatever issue we are dealing with.

It may sound cold or blunt, but by keeping your guard and check and not letting yourself get too close to someone upon meeting them, you can quickly avert any potential mishaps or crisis that may come forward within that relationship.

Being confident is your first step in averting a manipulative attack; depending on the type of manipulation used you are going to want to be confident in different areas.

The manipulation that a salesperson might use varies greatly from the type of manipulation a jaded lover would use on you, so knowing how to respond to each is paramount. For example, if you know a car is cheaper than someone is saying it is, be firm in your argument and do not let up ground. The same can be said if you suspect your partner of lying in a romantic relationship. By showing dominance in an encounter, you say to the manipulator that you are not someone who will fall for their bait; you will not be their plaything.

Moving on from just simply being confident and knowing your situation, there is de-escalation. Many manipulators, when confronted about their behavior, like to make the stakes of a situation seem higher than they are, with their end goal being that you will back off and drop the conflict out of fear.

Their goal is to scare you into submission through whatever means required.

Some will threaten suicide, some will threaten you directly, in the hopes you will back down. The trick here is to call their bluff and remain firm in your conviction that you know they are just trying to manipulate you.

Do not buy into their bluffs, as once a manipulator realizes they can get away with something once, they will do it again and again as you set a precedent for them that manipulative behavior is okay. Calling a manipulator bluff in a high-tension scenario like this, in the beginning may lead to them getting irater and more irrational.

But if you are firm and stand your ground, they will quickly come to terms with the fact that they will not win here.

The other component of de-escalation is not losing control of your own emotions - manipulators are very good at learning what buttons to press to set you off. Understand this when interacting with them, because if you just buy-in and get as angry and irrational as them, then you are stooping to their level and letting them get what they want from you, which is usually attention.

## CALMING TECHNIQUES

There are some simple calming techniques you can use when you feel your emotions brewing up. Take a slow deep breath and count to five in your head; you can also try peaceful imaging. Imagine yourself on a calm beach or somewhere pleasant to draw your mind away from the situation with the manipulator. Presenting yourself as calm shows a potential manipulator that you won't stoop to their level and are not willing to compromise your integrity.

De-escalation tricks are pointless if you do not take active steps to change things from there - this can be as simple as trying to set firm boundaries. The way you do this is that you let someone know what your limits are, what you won't put up with; for example, if someone lies to you and you catch them you are firm and consistent with the consequences. If establishing boundaries and trying to de-escalate the situation don't work, then it may perhaps be in your best interest to reduce the amount of contact you have with the manipulator.

Going low or no contact with a manipulator guarantees you that they cannot harm you. The problem with doing this is remaining firm in your conviction; it is very easy to tell someone that you are going to stop contacting them, but doing it is much more challenging.

Once a manipulator feels you are pulling away, they will ramp up their scheming in the hopes they can entice you into staying with them.

Simply put, leave them, block their number and possibly leave any friends you both share. Manipulators love to use other people to do their bidding. This allows them to act through proxies and avoid arousing suspicion that they are the ones responsible for certain behaviors. You may find that the more challenging part of reducing contact with someone who is a manipulator is the obstacles you set yourself.

Manipulators like to make you second guess yourself and doubt your instinct in the hopes that you will follow through with their intentions. This is why knowing certainly how you want to act is important. Take time to do your diligence before making any major decisions. Pull back for a little bit and analyze all the facts at your disposal.

By taking a calm and measured approach to your decisions and actions you present an image of someone who is not weak. This more than anything will prevent you from becoming a victim of manipulators' attacks. It represents the image that you are in control of your emotions and as a result can't have your own emotions used against you, as manipulators commonly try to get you to do.

In closing, know that you have a basic understanding of some of the methods manipulators use and how to defend yourself against them. You are now better able to understand where manipulation truly comes from and what drives people to use someone's own emotions against them. As a result of knowing how their weapons work, you can utilize them in tricky situations in life, where they may prove incredibly useful.

Because manipulation is so common in today's fast-paced world it is imperative for you to understand it if you want to get ahead. That is why I would like to discuss how psychological disorders play in manipulative behavior.

## MANIPULATION AND PERSONALITY DISORDERS

Since these personality disorders present themselves as continuous displays of abhorrent behavior it is easy to recognize them when you know the signs. The three most common disorders that make people prone to manipulative behavior are Antisocial Personality Disorder (APD), Narcissistic Personality Disorder (NPD), and

Borderline Personality Disorder (BPD). Understanding the pathologies and behaviors characterized by these kinds of psychological disorders allows you to quickly weed out people who could potentially be manipulators.

While it may seem cruel to avoid someone because they have a "disorder," when it comes to your wellbeing and security you can never be too careful.

## Borderline Personality Disorder

To begin the conversation on disorders that make one manipulative I would like to start with the lesser-known Borderline Personality Disorder or BPD.

BPD as a disorder is characterized by an intense pattern of instability in both interpersonal relationships and sense of self. This instability is accompanied by an extreme of abandonment which, when combined with the general impulsiveness and mood swings BPD brings, make for a perfect storm of destructive behavior. Since individuals with BPD have such an intense fear of abandonment they may lie and manipulate to keep you closer to them while at the same time getting angry at you for spending so much time with them. This splitting between their desires and fears is where the term borderline comes from; their emotions are always bordering on the edge. Ever so close to teetering off and having a nuclear meltdown but still so far away.

Often people with borderline personality disorder present their symptoms in a chaotic or disorganized fashion, which reflects the fact that they are unsure of who they are themselves. It is not known what causes an individual to develop a borderline personality disorder, but it is theorized that growing up in an abusive home or experiencing severe trauma at a young age makes someone more likely to develop it.

An individual with Borderline personality disorder may be able to lure you in with how they may appear to make themselves vulnerable.

They are prone to sharing intimate details of their life very early on in a relationship in the hope of establishing trust and moving the relationship along quickly.

This is where the instability in relationships comes into play; a person with a borderline personality disorder will want to move a romance or relationship much quicker than it should be. Their reasoning for this is their fear of being abandoned; this fear drives their whole being to such an extent that they will burn all their bridges in the ill-guided hope of keeping you. One of the final characterizations of BPD is a repeated pattern of intense tantrums and meltdowns when people leave them, for lack of a better word when this fear of abandonment ends up coming true due to self-sabotage borderlines have a bad tendency to self-destruct and burn down everything in their path.

Your best defense against a borderline is leaving before you are too involved. If someone wants to move a relationship quickly in a direction you don't feel comfortable with, then it is in your best interest to leave while you can and when you have not invested much emotion.

## Narcissistic Personality Disorder

Moving on from one of the least known disorders, I would like to discuss a disorder we have all heard of Narcissistic Personality Disorder or NPD.

NPD is characterized by extreme self-centeredness and an inability to comprehend and understand the consequences of one's actions. Because of this inability to understand consequences, narcissists tend to repeat the same self-destructive behavior over and over again.

We have all heard this term used to describe someone. Few of us actually understand what narcissism truly looks like. We are quick to label any behavior we don't like as narcissism when in reality it is subtler than that.

Narcissists are not the overt self-centered people the media likes to portray them as. A narcissist likes to utilize subtle tactics to get you to come in line with their way of thinking, as opposed to overt manipulation. By getting you to question your judgment, they can replace your ideas with theirs.

One of the main behaviors all narcissists exibit is the inability to take responsibility for their actions.

They will pin the blame for their actions on others instead of realizing that they are the reason misfortune keeps befalling them.

As a result of this inability to learn from past mistakes, the narcissist will often repeat the same behavior over and over again to try and meet the same goal. This is what makes them so dangerous - they are willing to go to extreme lengths to get their goals.

The largest danger from narcissists comes from what is called a narcissistic meltdown. When a narcissist feels cornered like an animal, they will meltdown and destroy everything in their path, even if it means damaging themselves. This can take many different forms; for some narcissists, this means something as extreme as suicide or even murder. Others may trash a lover's house when asked to leave the relationship. In short, when a narcissist realizes their game is up, they tend to blow a lot of fuses in their heads.

It is hard to postulate what motivates a narcissist to behave this way; current psychological research points to a poor sense of self. But the truth is it does not matter why they do something; what matters is your ability to avoid it.

Narcissistic manipulation mainly takes the form of what is called gaslighting, which in simple terms is the act of getting you to question your judgment of a situation and get you to think that you're the one with the issues and not them. By getting you to question your own beliefs regarding their behavior, a manipulator is then able to live rent-free in your head! This is extremely dangerous behavior because it allows for self-doubt to be reinforced and allows for the manipulator to instill dangerous thoughts and ideas into someone's head.

The main thing to look out for in someone who behaves like this is how they were in past relationships. If you see a pattern of them avoiding any responsibility for their actions, run away immediately.

## Gaslighting Narcissists

Manipulators can accomplish gaslighting through a variety of ways. The main method in which they try to manipulate you is by breaking you down over time, slowly wearing away at you with the same line of garbage over and over again till you are forced to believe it.

Once a narcissist has convinced you of their positioning it is very difficult to get a clear view. They obfuscate the truth and lie at every chance they have to try and get you on their side. They'll make you feel guilty for not going along with their behavior.

The fact that this happens slowly over time is what makes it so damaging; it becomes difficult for you to realize that the behavior you are being presented with isn't normal, and usually by the time you have realized it is already too late.

Narcissists are great at luring you back into their grips through very clever manipulation tricks; by subtly getting you to doubt yourself they slowly hook their tendrils into every aspect of your life until you feel powerless without them. The trick to getting past this kind of manipulation is just biting the bullet and running away. This can be hard to do because narcissists are very charming and good at convincing you they will change. But the truth is a narcissist is never going to change and their manipulative behavior is only going to get worse.

One of the narcissist's other dangerous weapons is to break down self-esteem in others. For instance, imagine you're an architect and you are working on a new model for a house. Your manager gives you the rough blueprint, in which you noticed there are a few areas that could use some improvements. You begin sketching your blueprint version and proceed to make a cardboard model of what they envisioned. A week later, your manager comes to see your progress, to which her face shows frustration. Raising her voice, she points out the designs different from hers, comments on how the rooms look too small and talks about how the deadline is in two weeks.

Situations like these where you are bombarded with criticism, make it difficult to figure out if what they're saying is constructive or destructive. Whichever one you decide it is, you want the person to get all their criticism out before trying to amend what you have done, since they will most likely ignore you while in such a state. Quietly take their words and wait until they're finished.

Afterwards, explain whatever changes you made and your reasons for doing so.

It is always good to know before being confronted if the change was worth it or not, so make sure to evaluate all your decisions. In any case, ask her to clarify her opinion. There is a good chance she will explain what she meant. However, if she were to dismiss your explanations and continue criticizing, at that point you can safely take her words with a grain of salt and realize that the comments may not be reflective of what is truly going on in the situation. Instead, consider that what she is saying may simply be an attempt to manipulate you and get you to do something she wants.

Accepting that you are in a destructive relationship with a narcissist can be a difficult thing to do, but once you start to look at all the signs together, it ends up making sense. Someone who is going out of their way to lie and get you to believe things only through their worldview is not someone you want to be with. That is perhaps the saddest part of the manipulation. It doesn't tend to change and happens to only get worse as time moves on. Taking this examination of a relationship to heart is required evil in the world we live in today.

# Typical Salesperson Manipulation Tactics

Perhaps arguably the most common form of manipulation in today's fast-paced society is the manipulation that salespeople will try and use on us. Most sales tactics play on simple human emotions such as need or desire and very specific fears like a fear of missing out or not belonging. Advertisements target us so subtly that we do not realize we are being taken for a ride until we make a purchase that we do not need. By using fancy colors and enticing cinematics, advertisements can play on very primal parts of our brain and get us to do what they want.

Look at the newest advertisements for the iPhone and how they show people who are happy while using their fancy brand-new iPhone. Are they truly happy because of their new iPhone or is it perhaps the situations they are shown in?

The first step any successful advertisement has to take in getting you to buy its product is to convince you that you need it. How can they sell you something if you don't need it? Simple, they do so by creating these huge social media marketing campaigns in which they show thousands of people lining up to buy the newest and greatest fancy phone. They can convince you that, if you want to be one of the cool kids, you should also buy into needing something you don't need at all, such as the new iPhone.

This manipulation works by playing on a psychological concept called "the fear of missing out".

Your fear of not keeping up with the curve will entice you to buy the product even if it sets you back financially and even if you don't need it. You may have noticed how in lots of stores the kid's toys are all colorfully lit and have cool and interesting cut-outs designed to catch the attention of your little tyke. These bright colors and exciting stimuli fire up the reward centers of our brains and get us primed to make a purchase.

The other trick salespeople will try and utilize is the "fake sale".

You are probably wondering what I mean when I say fake sales. Well simply put say an item has a sticker on it that says it was 15 dollars and is now ten dollars, you will assume that is on sale and if you buy it now, you're getting a good deal.

Well, the truth is much different than the reality you assume it to be - the item is always marked as "on-sale". By playing on this fear of missing out, salespeople manipulate you on a very primal and basic level, as such it can be hard to avoid and defend against.

Your best defense is knowing how much something is worth before you purchase it. Do your diligence and research prices of the item in question, shop around at different outlets to get an idea of what it is truly worth. This is especially important when purchasing a car, as the stereotypes about used car salespeople exist for a reason. They will tell you whatever you want to hear about a vehicle. Their main trick is trying to quickly get a read on you and discern your likes and dislikes; once they do this, they can lure you into thinking they're your friend. And a friend will always give you the best deal, right?

This is not always the case. The people who are in this industry are in it because they're good people-pleasers - they know what to say to people and how to get what they want from them. You can utilize some of these tricks in your own life - the main thing to remember when interacting with someone is to make them feel validated and special. By doing this you get their trust, and from there, you can go far. Feeding into the fact that car sales are mostly a trick. There is also real estate where a realtor will try to convince you that something you're going to invest in will only grow in value and you are missing out by not purchasing it.

They will try to woo you with stories about how great the local farmers market is and how their produce is so fresh, or how the schools in the area are so highly rated, but the truth is these things are usually just embellishments or flat out lies. One thing you may have noticed when looking at a potential house to buy is how the realtor may have baked cookies or how there will be premade candies or cakes. This is to get you to believe that the house is lived in, and this also plays on strong mnemonic cues. Humans associate smells strongly with emotion; as a result, we are quick to dismiss logic, and we will just go with our heart and ignore the facts.

All manipulation shares this idea of selling us a fake good, the end goal is the only thing that differs.

Now that we have gone over how to deal with manipulation in relationships, I would like to dive deeply into how the media uses manipulation to get us to purchase things or even sway our opinion and how we can protect against it.

Take the mainstream news in the United States for example. Instead of reporting on simply just the news and events around the world, certain news outlets will be composed of nothing but talking heads and editorials giving their opinion on everything. In a sense, they are trying to get you to think the way they want; whether this is out of malice or simple incompetence is up for debate.

But the crux of the issue is that when a news story is reported today, it is no longer simply just "news" - it is filled with many different people's opinions. And depending on the political leaning of the news outlet they may not report on other things. Another more damaging example of this kind of manipulation can be seen in social media such as Instagram and Facebook. And that is in the realm of the influencer, someone who is paid to present a false lifestyle and show off how certain products, whatever they may achieve, helped them attain it.

This form of manipulation preys on a common psychological trope called the fear of missing out. When we see these people living super blessed lives and how they have everything one could want, we start feeling bad about ourselves and, as a result, will go out and buy these products in the vain belief that they will help us live the same kind of blessed life. The truth is that all sales try to get us to assume that our lives will be better with whatever product they are pitching.

Now that we know this, how can you better equip yourself so that you do not fall victim to frivolous purchases of things you do not need? The first step in avoiding this type of manipulation is to take a glance back and realize that what people post on social media is what they want you to see. In the same mindset, what manipulators tell you is what they want you to hear.

With that knowledge, you can better keep yourself from being swayed. The second thing to understand is that, if you do happen to decide to go and purchase the products, do research on them, do not go and just buy something because it has Kylie Jenner's name stamped on it with a bunch of fabulous claims.

Always remember the truism that extraordinary claims require extraordinary facts. From there you can truly make an informed decision if you want to purchase something or not. If you have concluded that what someone is posting is a pure promotion or the product is harmful, then drop that social media then and there; you're better off not following it, that will be your final solution if all else fails.

## Manipulation in Advertising

Jumping back to media manipulation I would like to also talk about how advertisements try to use the same trick as social media influencers in getting us to purchase things that perhaps we do not need.

These ads are created this way to drive home the point that you can attain more happiness if you buy these items.

This feeds in on our desire to be like others and also into our fear of missing out. This form of manipulation is also seen when we go to supermarkets with colorful ads and things that draw our attention from what matters. So your best defense against these forms of manipulation is to research something before you buy it.

Too often than not we get convinced to buy something on emotional impulse and then try to justify it later.

## Sometimes You Can Be Too Nice

This is how we get manipulated; we let our emotions override our logic and, as a result, make incredibly poor decisions. To defend against this when shopping or trying to buy something always have an idea of what it is you're buying and do not allow yourself to be swayed by mass advertising as if you do that you will be setting yourself up for a whole world of hurt and loss.

Moving on from how salespeople try to manipulate you, I would like to move back to emotional manipulation and how to defend against it. Some people will try to manipulate you within the confines of a romance while others, such as friends or family, will manipulate you within the confines of that already preexisting relationship. Simply put, it can be easier for your friends and family to manipulate you because they do not have the issue of trying to get you in a relationship with them.

## Does Your Family Take Advantage of You?

Relationships are common places to spot manipulation, yet the most unspoken relationship where manipulation persists is between family members.

In most cases, relatives won't speak up against one another because, since they're related by blood, they emotionally feel that it would be wrong.

Imagine this scenario - your cousin and his two children asked to move into your house, which you allow them willingly. After some months go by, you notice that he has stopped paying rent, doesn't buy his groceries or utensils; rather he uses your ingredients and your silverware.

## You are being used.

So you decide logically to bring up the fact that he is not carrying his weight in your house. You say "Hey cousin Tommy, I know you and your family have been hit by hard times, but if you are going to live within my home, you need to get a job and help contribute to bills and, you know, just carry your own".

Keep in mind that when you brought this fact up to your cousin you said it very calmly and reasonably. If your cousin responds with "Oh it's hard, working long hours at my job and school supplies for my kids. You understand right?" his response indicates that he has no incentive to pay any amount of money to you and they will continue leeching off you. By saying "You understand, right?" he is manipulating you to feel guilty for him and let him continue to abuse you and take advantage of you.

"No – What I understand is that you are not paying your expenses!"

Make it clear that he will have to pay rent and if you want to compromise, he will be allowed to eat your food. If not, he will have to buy his own.

# Chapter 7:

# How To Deal With A Manipulator?

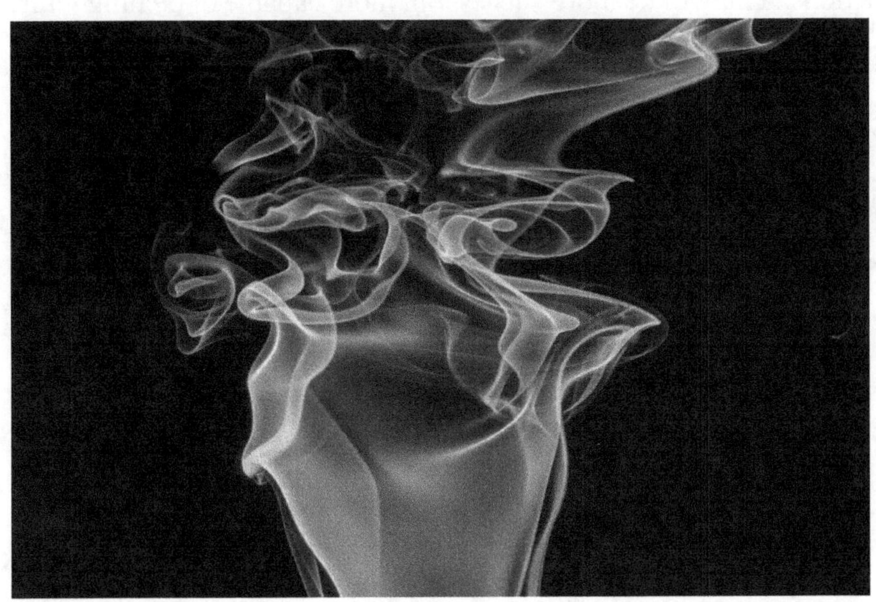



## Cut Them Off

When you are attempting to avoid a manipulator's antics, perhaps
the most successful method is by removing them from your life
entirely like the malignant cancer they are. By completely

separating yourself from the manipulator, you will find yourself far happier, rediscover yourself and your own thoughts and beliefs that have been suppressed all this time thanks to the manipulator's actions. You will be more successful, more capable of dealing with life and infinitely happier without that toxicity constantly raining on your parade.

## Ignore, Ignore, Ignore!

Manipulators want you to follow along with whatever they want you to do. They will say whatever it takes to get that reaction from you, even if their methods are cruel or hurtful. They may even make it a point to say things that you know to be blatantly untrue in hopes of getting you to react negatively or attempt to correct it. For example, they may make a snide comment at you, such as asking when the next baby is due. You could correct the person, calling out their awful behavior, or you could ignore it.

## Trust Yourself

Manipulators thrive off of convincing you that you do not know what is best. They may even go out of their way to make you doubt your own perception of the world, convincing you that you are wrong about inane details of life, until you are so convinced that you cannot see the world clearly that you default to the manipulator's decisions. Instead of listening to what the manipulator says is best for you, it is time to take back control and trust yourself.

## Beat the Manipulator at Their Own Game

Manipulators love to sneak into your life and slowly take over. They will take over your friends before systematically turning them against you. They may choose to point out how much of a failure you are because of some past mistake that is no longer relevant to anything you are doing just to put you down. They may find something that you want and constantly keep it just out of your reach for their own selfish thrills.

## Break the Habit

Sometimes, you get so caught up in the status quo that, even if you want to separate from a manipulator, you cannot get yourself out of the rut. You may find yourself suddenly missing the manipulator in your life, or something may happen that triggers a reaction that you did not expect. When this happens, recognize that the best step is to step out of your comfort zone and break the habits you have developed surrounding the manipulator. This does two things — it breaks your habituated response to obeying whatever the manipulator has conditioned you to do, and it also shows the manipulator that you are no longer going to tolerate their whims. The next time you feel the need to give in to what the narcissist expects, you should attempt something new.

## Do Not Expect Them to Agree with You

While you may hope that the manipulator will be rational if you try to speak to them or tell them how you feel, like normal, rational humans would do, you cannot expect the manipulator to actually learn anything from a confrontation. Instead, the manipulator will see it as ammo to use against you in any way possible, rather than as something that could be used as a learning experience. Instead of hoping that you can change the manipulator, cut your losses and move on. You will be far happier if you do so.

## Do Not Give in To Guilt

Guilt can be incredibly powerful—in fact, it is so powerful, it was likely used by the manipulator against you several times. Manipulators recognize the driving power of guilt when obligations are not met, and they utilize it well. However, you should not feel guilty for not living up to the manipulator's standards. You do not have to give in to the manipulator, nor do you have to give in to the manipulator's attempts to make you feel bad. Remember, recognize your innate human rights and utilize them. You are allowed to say no without feeling guilty.

## Never Ask for Permission

You are your own person. You do not need to ask the manipulator for permission to do something, nor should you ever feel the urge to do so. Instead of being concerned with the feelings of others, you should focus on disempowering the manipulator. They can only control you if you let them, and one of the ways you would hand over power is if you asked for permission.

## Learn the Signs

The easiest way to protect yourself is through ensuring you know how to recognize the signs of manipulators. Congratulations! You have already done this by reading through this book! As you learn what to look for, you know when something does not look right, and you will be able to question the other person.

## Never Ignore the Red Flags

You should NEVER ignore any red flags about the other person. If they are behaving in manipulative ways and you recognize that, you should not try to make excuses or give the other person the benefit of the doubt—they do not deserve it if they are manipulating you. Do not give in to any sob stories or anything else said to convince you to give in, and instead focus on the fact that you deserve better.

## Know all your fundamental rights

One of the single most imperative guidelines when you are in this similar situation is to know all your fundamental rights. But that's not all, you should also recognize when any of those rights are being violated. Remember that you are at liberty to stand up for yourself and make sure no single fundamental right is being violated. You should, however, do this carefully and make sure that you do not harm others. Again, you should not forget that you might forfeit these rights if you cause harm to other people. Ensure you are conversant with some of the basic human rights such as:

- The right to be treated with dignity and respect.

- The right to express one's wants, opinions and feelings.

- The right to give no as an answer and maintain that without any guilty feelings.

- The right to set up one's own standards and priorities.

- The right to take care and safeguard yourself from being emotionally, mentally, or physically threatened.

The mentioned basic rights show the extent to which your boundaries are supposed to reach. We are living in a society where people don't represent any of these rights. The mental manipulators are particularly interested in depriving you of your rights so that they can fully control you and take advantage of you. However, you still have the moral authority and power to state that you, and not the manipulator, are fully in charge of your life.

## Maintain a distance with these people

As noted, one of the surest ways of detecting a manipulator is to check if the individual acts with different faces when in front of various people and situations. Whereas all of us have mastered this art of social differentiation, the mental manipulators are masters when it comes to dwelling in extremes – where they show great humility to one person and rudeness to another. They can also feel so aggressive at one point and totally helpless the next minute. When you see this kind of behavior in people whom you are close to, the best thing to do is to keep a healthy distance. You should also try to avoid engaging with these people until you are really forced to do that. Remember that some of the top causes of chronic psychological manipulation are deep-seated and complex; therefore, saving or changing these people cannot be your job.

## Stop Self-Blaming & Personalization

Given that the manipulator's agenda is to know where your weakness is and exploit it, you may even throw the blame game on yourself for not doing your best. In such situations, it is very imperative to reassure yourself that you are not part of the problem. Remember that you are just being manipulated to feel bad about your actions and surrender your rights and power in the end. It is vital to consider the kind of relationship you have with the manipulator as well.

## Probe the Manipulators

Mental manipulators will always make demands or requests from you. They do this to make you go the extra mile so that you can meet their needs. At times, it can be very important to put the focus back on the manipulator each time you hear certain solicitations. Ask them some analytical questions to check if they are fully aware of their scheme's inequity. Ask them if their actions appear reasonable to them or if what they want from you is all fair.

## Say No in a Firm and Diplomatic Way

Saying no in a firm and diplomatic way is what can be defined as real communication. When it has been articulated in an effective manner, it will give you an opportunity to stand your ground and maintain the best working relationship. It is important to remember that one of your basic human rights is to set your own standards and priorities. It is also within your rights to say no without feeling the guilt, as well as the right to pick your own healthy and happy life.

## Set the Consequences

When a mental manipulator persists on violating the boundaries that you have made and is not hearing your "no," you will be forced to deploy the consequences. The ability to be able to point out and assert the consequences is one of the most important skills that you can deploy to resist the efforts of a manipulative person. When they are articulated in an effective manner, consequences will stop the actions of the manipulative person and even compel them to stop the violations and respect you instead.

## Confront the Bullies in a Safe Way

One fact that is not known to many is that a mental manipulator can turn into a bully when they intimidate and harm others. It is important to note that bullies only prey on those they regard as the weakest, and you can make yourself a target when you remain compliant and passive. However, the fact is that a number of bullies are cowards on the inside. They will often back up when their target starts to stand up for their rights. This is a common practice in office and surroundings, as well as in schoolyards.

## **Think about the long-term consequences of the actions you undertake**

As opposed to just doing what is easiest and fastest, do not forget about the consequences that your actions can have. Remember that psychological manipulators are the best when it comes to making their option the easiest, fastest, and also the least hurtful. They are also best at keeping the people focused on their current feelings. That explains why people do things they later regret. Instead of dealing with a consequence, later on, make sure you choose to do things that you won't be forced to rethink.

# Chapter 8:

## Are Manipulators Aware of Their Actions

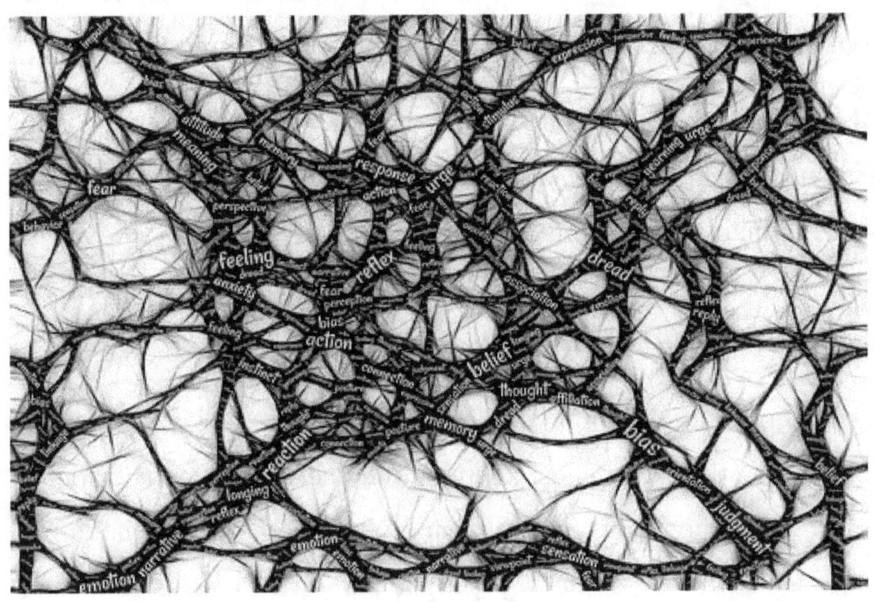

A successful manipulator should be able to have various ways or tactics at hand that will enable or make them succeed with ease in using people to get to their own final goals. There are numerous theories incorporated to achieve what makes a successful manipulator. Let's take a closer look at the 3 requirements to reach this goal. They are as follows:

A professional manipulator should be able to hide their wicked character from their subject, as it is one of the best techniques to reach their goal;

A good manipulator should be able to have a better knowledge of their subject, like how they feel when they are annoyed, how welcoming they are, who their friends are, what their capabilities in handling issues are and so on. Observations of this nature make it easier for the manipulator to thrive and get a desired result;

Manipulators are skilled and cunning; they have a word to back up every comment. They should always have a plan after reaching a goal, as their subjects might come after them. They are advised to have their minds ready against whatever outcome may surface, if the subject is harmed physically or emotionally.

The major thing a manipulator should do more if they want to excel in manipulating others is to keep or hold back their harsh character traits. They should be able to wear a smiling and accommodative face to help lure people who might perceive them as kind and welcoming.

Also, if the manipulator is talkative and goes around spreading their next plans, or is also harshly mannered when dealing with people, then nobody will find them worthy of influencing, which will hinder their goal. Instead, the manipulator needs to hide their plans from people and act as if all is well. In so doing, the victims will not know their intention until a reasonable result is reached.

The manipulator should be entertaining, jovial and helping. Before the subject could realize, the manipulator would have gathered enough information about them.

Also, the manipulator is supposed to have ideas on how to identify weak victims. These ideas will help spur them to achieve the required goals. The manipulator could sometimes achieve their result through observation, while at other times it may also require interaction with the subject before setting their plans.

Thirdly, the manipulator needs to be hardhearted. If they are bothered by the victim's feelings, then it will be difficult to achieve their aim. They should shut their mind against any harm which may befall their victims; how their subject will feel shouldn't be a burden to them. There are so many tactics available for them to deploy against their subject if they are truly eager for success - either physical or emotional technique could be the solution.

The manipulator's success lies in the ignorance of their victims, who would not realize in time, until it's already too late. It may seem okay to them, as they may see the manipulator as merely a friend, but before they could wake from their slumber, they would already be part of it, and there would be no going back because things would have gone beyond repair.

The manipulator will utilize various strategies, such as emotional blackmail, to handicap the victim.

# Chapter 9:
# Emotional Manipulation in A Relationship

## RECOGNIZING A MANIPULATIVE RELATIONSHIP

When thinking of love, our society romanticizes manipulative connections so much that it may be difficult to recognize them for what they are. We have loads of literature suggesting to us that genuine relationships are about fixation, that pure love is all-expending and that individuals who are infatuated have no personal limits or separate lives.

While many people romanticize the idea of a manipulative relationship, we have to understand that in reality, it is not real love. Sometimes it might make for a dramatic plot and conflict that keeps the reader invested, but there is no fun in actually living through a romantically manipulative relationship.

You may have been warned about manipulative people and the fact that control and maltreatment is something to be worried about; the facts are that being in a controlling and manipulative relationship that never grows into ill-treatment can be frightful and harming as well. Just because someone isn't physically harming you doesn't mean that you can't still feel pain from their actions.

Being controlled or put down by a companion can harm our confidence, make us feel dread about relationships in the future and leave us feeling abandoned instead of comforted, with an assortment of mental and emotional injuries that we should not be burdened with.

You might be acquainted with indications of a damaging relationship. For instance, you may have experienced a mate who compelled you to wear only certain items of clothing or did not want you to visit your friends and family.

This person might always want to know where you are going, what you are doing and why you are only a few minutes late. Manipulators are often very anxious people, so they will allow nervous thoughts to pass through their brains and control their actions. They will spiral their excessive emotion and anxiety into fantasies about what you could possibly be doing when you are not around them. They will think about their worst fears and what you could be doing to hurt them, so when you are not around, they are going to assume you are doing these things.

This can lead to them disliking that you are not around. It can seem flattering at times to have someone be so concerned with you. You might think, "It is so sweet that they always want to know where I am and that I'm safe," but when someone is going to great lengths to control you, this isn't their intention. Unfortunately, their concern isn't for your wellbeing. Instead, they are thinking, "I need to make sure I know where this person is at all times so that they aren't doing anything I don't approve of." Your presence is simply their assurance that you aren't fulfilling their worst fears about the bad things you are doing to them when the two of you aren't together. They won't be considerate of your needs in this situation. The manipulator is only acting to serve their own interests.

A manipulator will never tell you this and will instead only feign concern to improve the way they appear to you. They will also use this tactic to make sure that you feel guilty. When you don't answer for 20 minutes, rather than them admitting that it is completely acceptable for a person to not always text back immediately, they will make you feel guilty. They will treat you as if you have done something wrong or selfish to them, without considering the fact that you simply weren't around your phone at the time or were too busy to answer in the first place.

Love should feel better and not confining, terrifying or distressing, and having an accomplice should make you more joyful, not sadder. There are certainly going to be difficult times in love. You might not understand your mate, and they might not understand you. These challenges should be mere obstacles on the way to making you stronger. A healthy relationship shouldn't be one that is constantly draining you and breaking you apart, making you feel constantly exhausted.

## SIGNS OF A MANIPULATIVE RELATIONSHIP

A great deal of us have had awful stuff occur in our lives—enough awful stuff that the possibility of a hero sweeping us off our feet and shielding us from any issues for whatever remains of our life can sound incredibly enticing. For this reason, we sometimes seek protection, compassion, and care in the wrong places.

Reconsider if your partner's thoughts of help include preventing you from making your own choices and carrying on with your own life. A partner who secures you by assuming responsibility for your maxed-out accounts, or perhaps talking to a companion you've been battling with isn't paying special mind to you; they are attempting to make you have no other choice but to put all your trust in them and no one else.

A true partner realizes that they can't protect you from everyday life and what it holds— they can simply assist when you need them to. Should you, at some point, run into a money-related issue, a trustworthy partner may assist you in praying an overabundance of unopened bills—giving help, but not taking control over the situation. They won't take your passwords or demand that you only be allowed a limited amount of money per month until you have paid off all your current debt. A true partner will offer help yet will realize that you need to manage your own issues.

One common manipulative relationship tactic is to make us feel guilty for seeing friends and family members. When we envision somebody attempting to cut their companion off from their emotionally supportive network, we picture something similar to the contemptible husband in a made-for-television movie telling his better half that she'll never talk to her closest companion again. Be that as it may, manipulative partners can also separate you from your support network in an inconspicuous way.

A shrewdly manipulative person isn't going to outwardly forbid you from seeing your family because that can be an obvious sign that you should run in the other direction. They are going to make the manipulation subtler, instead pulling you from your family slowly rather than an outright forbiddance. If your partner can convince you to apologize for an action you know you did not do wrongfully, and you do, your manipulative partner will realize they can compel you to do anything they want you to do.

Perhaps your partner sulks each time you go out with your companions until you blow off other friends just to save yourself the pressure. Maybe your partner makes negative remarks about your loved ones until you start to trust that the thoughts they have about these people are valid.

You might even have a hobby or an activity that you enjoy that your manipulator will try to get you to stop doing. They will make sure you know they think your interest is idiotic and ridicule you for it until you surrender it.

A controlling partner's scrutiny might not always appear as such. It may be framed in reasonable and rational language that suggests your partner is merely attempting to help you. They may even tell you that they are simply trying to help you.

They may study your choices at work. Some of their phrases may include: "Why is it that you chose to use that for your presentation? Aren't you worried about what the boss is going to think?"

They will question your spending habits and how you choose to purchase things with questions like, "Did you really need to buy another shirt?" Manipulators will spin their words, so it isn't clear that they believe the choices you make are incorrect, but a seed of doubt and insecurity is planted.

However, all partners periodically scrutinize one another. Our loved ones should still look out for us, and sometimes we need others to help us make decisions or point out bad habits. Remember to always check the true intention of this person and figure out why they would actually want you to change your behavior.

Sometimes, a manipulator in a relationship might ask to have access to your personal belongings, but they won't give you the same privileges. They might know all of your secrets, yet they rarely confide in you. They aren't simply less likely to share, and they certainly aren't protecting you.

This type of behavior shows that the other person is being domineering. Your partner doesn't deserve the privilege to browse your email or messages or ask for your passwords since they state they are apprehensive of whether you may cheat. There's a distinction between having insider facts and having a healthy independence from your partner, and you don't need to surrender that when you are in a relationship with someone.

Every so often, genuine couples who are recuperating from an occurrence of betrayal will permit the undermined partner access to each other's messages as a type of accountability. Yet, in the event that this isn't an arrangement that you have explicitly worked out with your partner, it isn't right.

Manipulation is all about impacting the way someone else thinks and behaves, all through psychological control. This is masked with passion, or what seems to be a form of empathy, at least. Most of the time, this is a calculated attempt at relating to the victim by the manipulator in question.

In order to fully overcome this manipulation, it's essential that we can recognize the impact that it has had on us. If you want to have a healthy relationship with someone, it's crucial that we are looking at all the ways this relationship has affected us. If that impact is negative, it might be the first sign that a manipulative relationship exists.

Most manipulative people have four regular attributes:

- They know how to recognize your shortcomings.
- They utilize your shortcomings against you.
- Through their quick plots, they persuade you to surrender something of yourself to serve them.
- When a controller triumphs in exploiting you, they will probably repeat the offense until you put a stop to the mistreatment.

They will have many different reasons for why they want to keep you around and control you. One might be simply because they are damaged by a past relationship. They might have trust issues that have led to them having difficulty in being open and accepting of other partners. This can cause them to feel like they need to control you to keep you faithful to them.

Some partners might simply be lonely individuals who are desperate for love and attention. When they feel like you might take that way, or are fearful that you will leave them, they will stop at nothing to ensure you stick around, even if that includes manipulation.

They might also simply want practical things from you, like financial support, maybe your shared home, a car, and other privileges that aren't connected to you as a person whom they love, but rather the life that you choose to live. These are some of the most dangerous manipulators, and they are just as common as the rest.


**HOW TO DEAL WITH A MANIPULATIVE PARTNER**

## <u>Understand Your Rights</u>

When someone is in the middle of a manipulative relationship, it can be hard to understand how to get out. Manipulators are good at creating confusion, so they can often avoid immediate blame for trying to control others. The way to ensure that you are being protected is to remember your rights.

These are the things that you are absolutely entitled to and should never allow another individual to take away. If you can consistently remember these, it will be easier to confront manipulation as it is happening and more easily recognize when a conversation might be toxic.

Then again, if you convey vulnerability to other people, you may relinquish these rights. The following are our common, principal human rights:

- You deserve respect from others, especially those to whom you give respect.
- You are allowed to express your thoughts, feelings, and emotions.
- You reserve the right to understand your own needs, share those with others, and do what you have to in order to fulfill

those needs, so long as you don't take anything away from others.

- You reserve the privilege to state "no" without feeling regretful.
- You reserve the privilege to get what you pay for, work for and put effort toward.
- You have the right to protect yourself against other people if they are hurting you.
- You have the right to make your own cheerful and sound life.

Our general public is loaded with individuals who don't respect these rights. Mental controllers, specifically, need to deny you of your rights so they can try their manipulative tactics on you. However, you can push back against such attempts at control when you express the confidence and authority to announce that it is you, not the controller, who's responsible for your life.

These individuals have most likely bossed around others for such a long time and have never been stood up to for it. Please stand up for yourself and let them realize that they make you feel awkward and exploited.

Regardless of whether they deny their conduct or attempt to turn it back around on you, in any event, you can relax realizing you safeguarded yourself and took a stand for reality. Perhaps they will start to change their tune if they feel you hit a nerve with them; all things considered, when they frighten everybody off, they will have nobody to manipulate any longer.

Keeping a strategic distance from them is easier said than done if they don't demonstrate their genuine nature right away. Please heed the first indication of them steamrolling your feelings, gradually move in the opposite direction from the relationship, and make a point to tell them your limits.

Manipulators need another person to control, which is why they go to such desperate lengths to find people that they can influence. If you have been a part of a manipulative relationship in the past, they might be able to see some of that previous trauma as a way to make you more vulnerable to their advances.

If you notice that someone is consistently interested in your history and the negative experiences you've been through, consider that they are looking for your weaknesses and triggers. Some individuals might just want to relate to you on a more human level but be aware of the tactics that manipulators use to try and get a better control on their victims.

Some manipulators will routinely shift the person they can be from one situation to the next, being exceedingly courteous to one individual and totally inconsiderate to another or absolutely defenseless one minute and wildly forceful the following. When you see this kind of conduct from a person frequently, keep a healthy distance and abstain from engaging with the individual except for the most urgent needs.

No matter what the demand, there are some manipulators who will try to use the pressure of time and force you to make decisions quickly so that you don't have a chance to really consider what they are asking. On such occasions, rather than reacting to the controller's request immediately, think about utilizing time to promote your wellbeing and removing yourself from this manipulative grip. You can exert authority over the circumstance by making a simple statement such as "I'll consider it."

Think about how amazing these few words can sound to a manipulator. You have not committed to their demands, yet you do not deny them either. That gives a manipulator the sense that they already have power over you, although you know otherwise. Take the time you have to assess the advantages and disadvantages of a circumstance and think about whether you need to arrange a more fair game plan or take control and put yourself in an ideal situation.

Your essential human rights include the privilege to identify your own needs, the privilege to state "no" without guilt, and the privilege to choose what a fulfilling and stable life looks like. Practicing the act of saying "no" out loud enables you to rehearse clear and assertive communication. And to then say "no" to a manipulator, doing so with care yet immovably, gives you a sense of self-control while keeping the door open to the relationship.

A manipulator turns into a domineering jerk when the individual in question scares or damages someone else. Nothing can help reveal a true manipulator's intentions and feelings more then if they are forced to confront themselves and really look deep into the ways they are treating others.

The most crucial thing to remember about oppressive jerks is that they tend to scope out the individuals who seem likely to succumb to manipulation. Thus, if you keep confident, you won't fall as high on a manipulator's prospect list as others may.

Be that as it may, numerous harassers are defeatists on the inside. At the point when their victims start to demonstrate the authority to stand up for themselves, the domineering jerk will regularly withdraw. This is valid in social and school situations as well as in office conditions.

On a compassionate note, research proves that numerous harassers are casualties of brutality themselves. Yet this should not in any way pardon harassing conduct. Knowing that harassers have often been victimized may enable you to think about the domineering jerk in a more empathetic light. But remember that someone who is hurt shouldn't be hurting others. After you have been manipulated, does that mean you will go and do the same to someone else?

While going up against menaces, make sure to put on a brave face and stand your ground while having other individuals present to observe and stand with you when you need additional help. In instances of physical, verbal, or psychological mistreatment, don't be afraid to notify or consult applicable legal resources, law enforcement and health specialists.

It might seem dramatic to have an entourage with you, or even a police officer, when doing something like picking up old belongings from an ex-manipulator's home or meeting up with them. However, it is always worth protecting yourself. Though we can predict some of the thinking patterns of a manipulator, we never can truly know how they are going to react in any given situation.

## Don't Allow the Self-Blame to Take Over

Since the controller's motivation is to search for and abuse your weaknesses, it is understandable that you may feel deficient, or even scorn yourself for not fulfilling the manipulator's motives.

In these circumstances, recollect that you are not the issue; you are being manipulated to feel terrible about yourself, with the goal that you are bound to surrender your capacity and rights. Think about your association with the controller, and ask the following questions:

- Is this person being considerate of my basic human rights?
- Is what they are asking me to do reasonable, fair and something that I can achieve without hurting myself?
- Are they asking this of me because they can't do it or because they don't want to do it?
- Are both parties in this relationship giving, or is it only coming from one end?

- Do I like the person that I am when I am around them? Are they their best version when they are around me?

Your responses to these inquiries give you critical hints about whether the "issue" you find yourself in is a result of something you are doing or something your partner is doing.

Another thing you can do to protect yourself from manipulators is to put a target on their back by asking questions. Always make them answer their own questions and force them to self-reflect on their behavior.

Manipulators base their attempts at control in getting you to do the things you don't want to do. It's as simple as that. These offers regularly influence you to make a special effort to address their issues. Should they say or suggest something that sounds unfair, makes you uncomfortable or is unreasonable, it is important to return the emphasis to the controller by asking a couple of questions to check whether they have enough mindfulness to perceive the imbalance of their plan.

When you are asking the above questions, you are setting up a silhouette of what the manipulator expects of you. That way, the manipulator can see precisely what their behaviors are masking. In the event that the controller has a level of mindfulness, the individual will probably excuse their offensive behavior and state what they want in a more constructive way.

Then again, expert manipulators will dispel your questions and demand getting their way. If this happens, take note of the next tips that we discuss to get out of a manipulative situation.

## Set the Consequences

At the point when a manipulator demands something that transgresses your limits, make the consequences of their actions known. Ensure that you are always sharing your feelings, because these they cannot deny. They might not understand your feelings. Nor will they always be willing to listen. And don't expect them to offer up sympathy.

However, they can't say that your feelings aren't true. If they do, then they are gaslighting you, which is an abusive tactic that you should never stand for. When you are forcing them to really consider the way that they made you feel, it can help to show the consequences. Even if you forgive them internally, don't show it right away. Wait for them to exhibit the changed behavior that you have been asking for.

Let's look at one example. Let's say your partner manipulated you into skipping your family party because they didn't want to go, and they didn't want you to go without them. Let them know that they hurt your feelings and that they made you feel bad about missing your family. They might say, "No I didn't," but they don't get to decide this.

You can let them know that you understand that might not have been their intention (even though it likely was), but that you were still hurt either way. If they aren't willing to accept this, why are you willing to accept that they were hurt when you were considering going to the party without them? Ask this question. If they are not willing to listen to your feelings, why should you be willing to listen to theirs?

Do not give in to them, no matter how hard they try, until they recognize that they hurt your feelings. It's as simple as that. They might try to avoid it, make you laugh, or distract you so that you aren't mad, but do not give in until they admit they hurt you and apologize for it.

The capacity to distinguish and declare consequences is one of the most critical aptitudes you can use to deal with a troublesome individual. A consequence is something that is going to hurt them, not you. Ask yourself what you can take away from them to really get them to start thinking about you, and not just themselves in any given situation.

Another example of manipulation might be your partner giving you the silent treatment after you have ignored them for an hour. Let's say that you were at work and you got busy, so of course you missed their message asking what you wanted to watch on TV later that night. This is a very simple thing and a reasonable scenario. You can't be expected to answer your phone every minute of the day, especially when you are tending to work responsibilities.

When you get home, your partner is locked in the bedroom, not talking to you at all. They are ignoring you and aren't willing to listen to you. This makes you feel bad and you start to question if something is wrong with you. If they are lying in bed, then you are thinking they must've been upset all night and you might start to feel really guilty about what you did, even though you did absolutely nothing wrong.

Rather than giving in to them and apologizing over and over, they should really be the one apologizing to you! In this situation, you should sit down on the bed and tell them that you were busy at work which is why you weren't able to respond. Let them know you would still enjoy watching something. If they don't immediately change their mood and continue to throw a pity party for themselves, simply walk away.

They are looking for an emotional reaction. They want to know that they successfully controlled you. Don't give in to this. They need to reflect and realize that the only person responsible for that bad mood was themselves. If they were legitimately concerned about growing with you, then they would accept that you weren't able to answer and talk about their feelings with you.

The silent treatment is a manipulative tactic aimed at making you feel guilty, so you will submit to their control. Seize the control of your evening in this scenario. Go watch a movie alone, leaving them in bed to be angry.

## **<u>Maintain your distance</u>**

Yet another way to identify a deceiver is to see whether a person is acting differently in various situations and around different individuals. While we all have a level of this kind of social differentiation, a few psychological tricksters strive to habitually linger in extremes, being extremely polite to one person and totally scary to another — or totally helpless at one instant and ferociously violent at the next. When you regularly witness this sort of behavior from an individual, maintain a good distance, and avoid interacting with the individual unless you absolutely have to. As described earlier, there are nuanced and deep-seated causes for persistent psychological abuse. Changing or saving these is not your job.

## **<u>Put your spotlight on them by posing questions</u>**

Psychological manipulators can eventually render inquiries (or demands) to you. Perhaps these "offers" force you to go out of your way to satisfy their desires. When you encounter an unfair argument, it is often helpful to bring the emphasis directly on the manipulator by posing a few inquiring questions and see whether they have sufficient self-awareness and understand their scheme's inequity. For instance:

- "Do you think this is sensible?"
- "Do you sound realistic on what you want from me?"
- "Do I get to have a say in this regard?"
- "Are you informing me or asking for my consent?"

- "What am I getting out of this, then?"

You're holding up a mirror as you pose these queries, and the trickster will see the real essence of their trick. If the deceiver has a sense of self-awareness, they are likely to retract the query and back down.

On the other hand, truly compulsive manipulators (such as a narcissist) will reject your questions and insist on getting their way. If this happens, apply ideas from the below-mentioned tips to keep your power and stop the manipulation.

### Know how to say "no" in a strong way.

Practicing the ability to communicate effectively is to be able to say "no" tactfully but strongly. Expressed effectively, it lets you hold your ground whilst still maintaining a functional relationship. Note that basic human rights include the freedom to choose yourself, the ability to tell "no" without feeling bad and the freedom to have your own comfortable and safe existence.

### Using Resources to Your advantage

In addition to unfair demands, the manipulator would often also demand an immediate response from you, to increase their power and influence over you in the case. At such times, instead of instantly reacting to the manipulator's appeal, try using the time to your benefit and detaching yourself from its immediate impact. You can learn to take control of the situation by simply saying

## "I'm going to think about it."

Take into account how effective these few words are from a client to a sales representative, from a romantic point of view to a keen pursuer or from you to a trickster. Take a moment and evaluate a situation's pros and cons and take into account whether you want to negotiate a fairer agreement or whether you're better off saying "no," which leads us to the next aspect:

## Confront Bullies Confidently

A psychological trickster turns into a bully when they frighten or harm someone else.

The most crucial factor to bear in mind about troublemakers is that they pick those they interpret as weaker, and as long as you stay passive and compliant, you become a target for them. However, a lot of bullies are cowards on the inside. Once their targets start displaying courage and sticking up for their interests, the abuser always turns away. This is true both in schoolyards and in the home and work environments.

Studies reveal, on an empathetic basis, that often abusers are themselves targets of abuse. This does not justify abusive conduct in any way, but may make you view the bully in a more enlightened manner:

- "When individuals don't really like themselves, they have to cover up for it. Actually, the classic bully was a victim first. "

- "Some individuals try to be tall by slicing other people's heads off."

- "I learned that bullying never has anything to do with the victim. It's the bully who has underlying insecurities. "

When handling threats, make sure to place yourself in a role in which you can defend yourself comfortably, whether it's standing alone, getting multiple witnesses there to watch and help or maintaining a written record about the offensive actions of the bully. In situations of physical, mental or emotional harassment, communicate with counselors, police departments or administrative staff.

## **Set repercussions**

If a psychological trickster insists on breaching your boundaries and is not going to take "no" for an answer, implement consequences.

One of the most valuable techniques you may utilize to "back up" a challenging offender is the willingness to recognize and demonstrate consequence(s). Correctly expressed, consequence allows the deceptive entity a pause and causes them to move from abuse to appreciation.

## SHAMING

The sole aim of the manipulators is to make the subjects feel uneasy and also to pity the subjects into believing the manipulator's act, to enable them to achieve their goals. They use sarcasm as a technique to body-shame the subjects to feel inferior. The shaming tactics include subtle sarcasm, harsh voice, a fierce look and so on.

## MANIPULATORS WANT YOU TO FEEL REJECTED

Sometimes manipulators will wait until the perfect moment before they try to help you. For example, they might sit back while you are both at the bar and wait for someone to reject you. When this happens, they will quickly come to you and try to make you feel better. They might tell you that the person was dumb to reject you because you are beautiful. They will try to build up your confidence so you will start to believe them and allow them into your life.

## LYING BY OMISSION

They will tell some unnecessary truth and keep the vital ideas to themselves. For instance, the manipulator may tell you they need some money to cut their hair, whereas, what they intend to use the money for is to buy cigarettes. In this scenario, you can see that the real truth wasn't told because the victim wouldn't have given the money for such use which could implicate them.

## DENIAL

Manipulators never admit that they are at fault even when they are caught red-handed. They will try to deny no matter how much you persuade them to say the truth. Rather, they will find a means to put the blame back on you.

## RATIONALIZATION

Here, the manipulator will make excuses that look too good to be true to confuse their subject. They will say or do so to spur happiness or delight in the mind of their subject. For instance, they may say they did it to favor the subject, whereas it is just an act done to cover their game. This is also similar to the spinning technique.

## MINIMIZATION

This is an addition of rationalization and denial techniques altogether to manipulate their subject. In this case, the manipulator will tell people not to believe the subjects who think of them as wicked or that their act is not as disgusting as the subject thought. For instance, the manipulator may insult their subject and call it a joke. And still expect the victim to believe them wholeheartedly.

## SELECTIVE ATTENTION OR INATTENTION

In this technique, manipulators try to avoid anything that will hinder them from achieving their desired goals. They will overlook every attempt of attention, as if they are not concerned. They will say "I'm not ready for that now," "I will talk to you later," "Please let's have the discussion next time" and so on, although in reality they are not concerned. What they are after is their result.

## DIVERSION

Manipulators are not just liars; they are experts at turning questions to their favor. They also try to avoid direct replies to questions when asked as much as possible. For instance, if their subject wants to ask questions that may spur them to know their fate. Whether they are lying or not, the manipulators will prefer to give a harsh or uncandid reply, or better still, change the topic of discussion to something inconsequential to curb the vital information that could leak their secret to the subject, as it will be harmful to them.

## EVASION

This technique is a little related to diversion. Here, the manipulator answers all questions thrown at them using harsh and rambling voices, murmuring to disconnect the subject's attention. In the end, the subject may have more questions to ponder on, rather than answers.

## INTIMIDATION

The manipulator most times tends to use intimidation to stir fear and threat in the mind of their subject. They will try to protect their subjects in order for them to remain within their clique of friends throughout the period needed to reach their goals. This is done using subtle, indirect, implied, veiled threat to make a fool of their subject.

## GUILT TRIP

The manipulators like to use this because it works perfectly for them. Here, the manipulators will say all sorts of things to make the subject feel guilty. They will intimidate them using various phrases, like, "is very selfish," "is not accommodative," "is not my kind of person," or even, "pay no attention to them." This will make the victim anxious, uneasy and willing to find a way back to being submissive in order to impress the manipulators. The subject will then be kept in a bad or self-doubting mood, which makes it easier for the manipulator to exploit them and reach their desired goal.

## MANIPULATIONS CREATE DISTRACTIONS

Creating a distraction is a common form of manipulation that many people use, such as political parties, public personalities and governmental leaders. This is a common technique used when someone wants to divert your attention away from the main issue. They will create a distraction on a smaller issue and make this out to be the larger problem. This will cause you to pay attention to the distraction, allowing the manipulator to do what they want.

## MANIPULATORS WILL MAKE YOU FEEL OBLIGATED

Manipulators are quick to do you a favor. This is because they are trying to get you to feel like you are indebted to them. Think about it - when someone does something for you, don't you feel like you need to return the favor? After all, it is only common courtesy, correct?

While you might feel this way, a manipulator is going to see an avenue for them to trap you into doing something for them, whether you will truly want to or not. For example, your friend bought you tickets to the concert you wanted to go to but couldn't afford. A few months later, your friend asks you to do something for them. While their request makes you a bit uncomfortable, you agree because you remember they purchased those tickets and didn't ask you to pay them back. Therefore, you owe them a favor.

## PLAYING THE VICTIM

The manipulator will try to show that they are the victim, even though they are the ones in charge of affairs. They act like the victim of the circumstance to evoke sympathy and pity through their expressions, even though they are not the ones affected. People who fall into this trap will be brainwashed to cooperate with them.

## VILIFYING THE SUBJECT

This is a superior technique used by the manipulator which puts the subject on the defense side of the matter, to keep the subject safe and, at the same time, hide the harsh intentions of the manipulator. The manipulator will then turn the situation to suit themselves. They will make the subject appear like the bully. The subject will want to calm the mood and expression of the manipulator, making it simpler for them to be exploited.

## SEDUCTION

Manipulators can also use seductive techniques to achieve their aim. Some of the tools that fit in here are behaviors like praise and charm, intense support and flattering of the subjects. This is to make the subject open-minded to them or lower their defense towards them. Within a short time, the subject will succumb to the manipulator by being loyal and trustworthy, who will then use them to achieve their result.

## PROJECTING THE BLAME

The manipulator will fancy blaming people for the problems they committed by themselves. They are trained liars who know when to act without being caught. Manipulators do all these things to the subject knowing they can't detect them due to their level of ignorance. Most times it is difficult to even know when the act is going on, so nobody will expose them.

## BLACKMAIL

Blackmail is the first tactic of the manipulator. It's the process of using threats to reveal false or true information about someone, which is often damaging because of intended gain. Here, the manipulator uses this means to oppress the subject to meet their demands. They pose threats like taking the subject's property, kidnapping the subject or prosecuting them as criminals. They don't retire unless their demand is reached.

Manipulators use this style to get their result. They spy on the intended persons for a while before unleashing their plans to blackmail them as they have known much. They could blackmail their subject using several strategies such as threatening to reveal a secret, standing against a chance of being promoted at work and so on, if they don't yield to their will. Whichever tactic the manipulator deploys, it is to achieve their selfish desire using the subject.

## Surrendering to the Other Person

However, if the manipulator must achieve their major objective, they have to make sure to explore many of the available options. One very functional way for successfully achieving this feat is being able to surrender to the other person and putting them down. If verbal skills are to be employed, the manipulator risks making the subject feel the effects of the personal attack on them. The moment they start getting this feeling, they tend to bristle off and fail to help the manipulator achieve their goals as they are more inclined not to like the manipulator at all.

## Creating an Illusion

Just like lying, manipulators are determined experts in creating illusions in such a real way to efficiently hone their goal. They try to create an elusive image that can convincingly make any picture seem very real. Normally, manipulators are not overly concerned on how it affects the subject. To effectively do this, the manipulator would try all within their power to build formidable evidence to prove their point.

To begin with, the manipulator starts by planting evidence and ideas in their subject's mind, and the moment this is perfectly done, the manipulator can safely sit back and allow the ploy planted to work on the mind of the subject. Once this is done the chances of maneuvering the subject into falling into their plan will increase.

## FEIGNING INNOCENCE

When a manipulator is caught in the act, they act innocent to save face. If harm was done to the subject, they may say it was unintended. They may even deny being involved in the situation by wearing a look of surprise to make the victim question their sanity, as if they had accused the wrong person.

## FEIGNING CONFUSION

The manipulator in this aspect tries to act unconcerned when exposed for their act. They will even claim knowing nothing about the situation when they are asked. They may appear confused when a critical question which demands an answer is asked.

## BRANDISHING ANGER

The manipulator uses anger to gain sympathy and pity from the subject. Though the manipulators are not truly angry, the anger may come in the form of them squeezing their face, snubbing their subject, or even answering them with a hard voice. All these tactics are just bait they may deploy to bring the subjects into submission. If this technique becomes effective, then the manipulator's goal is achieved.

# Chapter 11:
## Manipulation Tactics

## FOOT IN THE DOOR TECHNIQUE

The foot in the door technique is probably one of the most well-known forms of manipulation. It is also considered to be one of the oldest. It dates back to when people used to go door to door trying to sell their product. Of course, the salespeople took the phrase a bit more literally than manipulators. While salespeople would literally place their foot in front of the door so the homeowner couldn't close it on them, manipulators take more of a mental and emotional stance towards this technique.

The first step manipulators use is by asking for a small favor or "breaking the ice" through a small conversation. This helps the manipulators build a rapport with their target. For example, if they are trying to find a significant other, they will find a way to become compatible with their target. They will then ask the person questions about what they like and mention they enjoy the same things.

This technique is often how people get to know each other in a social setting. For example, have you ever been sitting at a club or coffee shop when someone came up to you and started small talk? They might have stated it was a busy night or a nice day. You might have agreed in some way, whether verbally or through your actions. Giving a reaction is letting the person keep their foot in the door. While you are probably just trying to be polite, depending on their motive, they see it as a step into your life.

## NEGATIVE REINFORCEMENT

Master manipulators will often use a tactic called negative reinforcement in order to get you to stop doing something they don't like. This could be anything from going out with your friends, going back to college or getting a job. Typically, they don't like anything that leads to a loss of control and threatens their environment.

When you start to do something they don't like, they will do something that you don't like. This is the first step of negative reinforcement. They will continue to use negative reinforcement, along with other tactics to try to get you to stop doing what they don't like. Once they have manipulated you to stop, they will then stop.

Another way that negative reinforcement works is when the manipulator starts to do something you don't like because you won't do what they want you to do. In order to get the manipulator to stop doing what you don't like, you have to do what they ask of you, even if you don't like it.

The main reason negative reinforcement is used is that it makes it more likely that you will do what they ask of you in the future without hesitation. This is especially true for manipulators who use any type of abuse to get you to stop doing something or to listen to them.

## THE EMOTIONAL TRIANGLE

The emotional triangle is similar to a love triangle; however, it is used against you. The manipulator will use it in order to get you to do what they want. They will create a triangle with themselves, you and a third person who is not directly involved in your relationship.

The manipulator will not hide the fact that they are interested in the third person, even if they aren't in truth. They will flirt with the person in front of you and even show affection toward the person. Sometimes they will use certain affections that you like, whether it is rubbing the person's back or giving them a hug.

While it might be obvious they like the other person, they will deny any type of affection in a confrontation. They will blame you, telling you that it is your insecurities and low self-esteem which is making you believe this.

The main goal of the emotional triangle is for you to become insecure about your relationship, which means you will work harder to make your significant other happy. You will do what they ask, even if you don't want to or feel uncomfortable taking on the assignment.

### ESTABLISHING SIMILARITIES

The foot in the door technique can often lead manipulators into another technique where they establish similarities. This is similar to the previous example; however, it is usually stronger than asking a few questions. For example, the manipulator might learn through observation or from a friend that you like a certain coffee shop. Therefore, they will decide to run into you at the coffee shop, where they discuss how much you both enjoy the location and the coffee.

Manipulators will also mirror your actions. They will notice if you are putting your elbows on the table and do the exact same thing. They will notice your hand gestures and how often you smile. They will then mirror these actions as well. This is a psychological tactic that reaches into your subconscious mind. It makes you feel like you can trust the person because you feel more connected, even if you don't realize they are mirroring your actions and behaviors.

# FEAR-RELIEF TECHNIQUE

Fear is a strong emotion and can often cause us to react in extreme ways. People are typically uncomfortable with fear, which means they will want to find a way to ease their fears. Because of this, manipulators commonly use the fear-relief technique as it allows them to gain the trust of their target by using emotion.

This technique is heavily used by manipulative people who create a fear in you so they can give you relief, which makes you more likely to listen to their requests next time. For example, you and your significant other have a disagreement that makes you leave the house and go for a drive or to a friend's house to vent. You come home and your significant other is gone. You wait a couple of hours and when they still don't return, you call their cell phone. They don't pick up. Another hour later, you try calling them again but receive their voicemail. At this point, you start to become anxious about the situation. You have left dozens of text messages and they don't answer their phone. You start to worry that something has happened to them. A couple of hours later they send you a text that says they are on their way home and everything is fine.

When you confront your significant other as they walk in the door about what they were doing, they respond that you left, so they could too. They then tell you that as long as you do something like that to them, they can do it too.

## MANIPULATORS WILL PUT YOU ON THE DEFENSE

Manipulators like to reach into your emotions because they are powerful. When you react with your emotions, you stop thinking clearly, make irrational decisions and have trouble remaining calm. This is how a manipulator wants you to react, because conversations where you think rationally and are calm do not go in their favor.

Therefore, manipulators use a tactic where they put you on the defense. This means that you will feel like you need to explain yourself. You have to defend how you feel, who you are and what you believe. This is one of the strongest signs of manipulation, but one that people don't often notice because it becomes common.

## GASLIGHTING TECHNIQUE

Gaslighting is phrasing the manipulator will use repeatedly in order to make you believe a situation you remember is wrong. Some of the most common phrases include "You can't be serious," "I never said that," "You don't remember it correctly," "Are you crazy?" and "You are imagining it." While you might feel that you are right, the manipulator will continue to stand by what they say, believe, or even give you their version of the situation. They might mix gaslighting with other tactics in order for you to start questioning yourself. They will continue to break you down through gaslighting or simply find a way to end the conversation.

Gaslighting is a very dangerous tactic because it is used to distort your reality. If it is used enough, you might start to feel that you are crazy, or you imagine all these situations. This will mentally and emotionally break you down even further, which will allow the manipulator to gain the upper hand as you start to distrust your own thoughts, emotions and abilities. You start to distrust your reality, making you believe that you are not seeing what you see, and you do not actually hear what you hear.

## TRAUMATIC ONE TRIAL LEARNING TECHNIQUE

Manipulators are good with putting on an act. They don't always mean what they say or how they feel, but they will get you to believe that they do. One technique that manipulators use to get you to listen to them better so they can keep you under control easier is called traumatic one trial learning.

When a manipulator uses this technique, they will become angry when they feel you have done something wrong. For example, if you come home later than you said you would, your significant other might yell, make you feel ashamed or become verbally abusive. They will act in a way they know will make you fear their anger, so you are less likely to do something like that again.

## MANIPULATORS WILL REFUSE TO DISCUSS CERTAIN TOPICS OR BEHAVIORS

For a manipulator, this is often looked at as a defense mechanism. They will absolutely refuse to answer any questions that put them in a bad light or put their behavior in question. While they will try other tactics, such as excuses, making you feel guilty or blaming you, if nothing else works for them, they will directly end the conversation. Of course, if you continue to try to push them for answers, the way the manipulator will act varies. They could become violent, which is why people always suggest that you need to watch their temper and behavior before you continue to push them for answers. If they are getting to the point where they might physically assault you, it is time to step away and leave.

## SMEAR CAMPAIGN TECHNIQUE

There are times when a manipulator can't break you down emotionally and mentally to the extent they would like. This means that you don't allow them to destroy your confidence and self-image. You might realize that they are manipulators, or you might not believe them for other reasons.

But just because they can't break you down, doesn't mean that won't try a different tactic. The smear campaign is when the manipulator will chip away at your image in a more social setting. They will start slandering your public image and ruining your reputation. They will do this through a variety of ways, such as bullying, sarcasm or making up stories about you that portray you negatively. They will work to label you as the toxic person and get people to believe that they are the victim.

## CREATING FAKE INTIMACY

One of the first steps a manipulator will take is getting you to trust them. This will allow them into your life a bit easier. It will also psychologically tell you that you can let your guard down as this person will not hurt you.

The best way manipulators do this is through a false sense of intimacy. They will tell you something private, sometimes stating they have never told anyone this before. Many manipulators will use emotions in order to gain your trust. For example, a manipulator might tell you about a time they were abused as a child or growing up with an alcoholic parent. These stories can be full of details that will make you feel sorry for them. While some manipulators might tell you a real story, some will make something up. They might tell the same story to all of their victims.

## ATTENTIVELY LISTEN

Listening is a tactic that manipulators often use. This is because it often works in their favor. Think about how important you feel when someone is closely listening to you. You start to feel like they truly care, and you start to trust them. Listening opens the door for a manipulator to step into your world.

## MANIPULATORS REMAIN UNPREDICTABLE

Manipulators might catch on to you feeling that they are becoming boring or feel you are catching on to their patterns. When this happens, they will switch gears quickly, doing something unpredictable to leave you guessing about their behavior.

Staying unpredictable will also make you feel that they are fun and exciting. This will make you want to hang out with them and learn to trust them. This is another way that manipulators get you to open the door for them so they can become a part of your life.

This is why manipulators tend to get some of the best and most unique gifts. When they are in a romantic relationship, they don't often go for regular gifts. Instead, they will give their significant other something more personalized, such as a book of poems, a gift card, a book or music.

## MANIPULATORS WILL TRY TO SILENCE YOU

Manipulators don't easily give up when they find someone fighting against their techniques. This just means they need to up their game, or as some people say, put you in your place. They will do this through a variety of means from verbally and emotionally abusing you to physically abusing you. They might also do this in more subtle ways, such as giving you the silent treatment or another form of punishment.

## EMPTY WORDS AND INTENTIONALLY FORGETTING

Manipulators are quick to make promises or commitments to you. They might agree that they will do something with you one night, but never follow through with it. This is a common tactic they use known as intentionally forgetting.

It is important to remember that when manipulators tell you they love you, they want to be with you, they support you, they won't hurt you, or they will do anything to make you happy they are lying. They are using empty words which mean a lot to you, but nothing to them. Therefore, when they intentionally forget to follow through with a promise, they don't feel bad as they never meant to follow through with the promise.

They also don't care how this has made you feel. They might act like they feel guilty or care that they hurt you, but once again, they are just saying words they know you want to hear. Unless their words are going to benefit them in any way, they do not mean what they say.

## MANIPULATORS WILL LEARN YOUR KEY PHRASES

Everyone has certain phrases or words which will lead them to take action. For example, someone who is against racism will pay more attention to a conversation when the words "racism" or "inequality" are used. This is because they are passionate about this topic. Furthermore, if they are a social advocate, they want to know what is going on so they can find out how they can help.

Manipulators will learn your keywords, so they know when to say or when not to say them. If they want you to do something, they will more likely tie their request in with your keywords. If they don't want you to do something, they won't use the keywords.

Of course, there are words that tend to be keywords for nearly everyone. For example, most people feel certain emotions when they hear the words "love," "trust," "hope" and "security." This is because these words often fill us with the positive emotions that our bodies crave. Everyone needs to feel these words in their life. Therefore, when a manipulator uses these words, you are more likely to feel comfortable and trust them. You feel that they are a good person and someone you can let your guard down with.

## MOVING GOAL POST TECHNIQUE

By now, you realize that a manipulator never truly has your best interest in mind. They might act like they do, and you might believe they do. However, they are also constantly trying to move closer towards their goal post, which is their ultimate target of control.

To do this a manipulator knows they have to act like they are your best friend, they love you, want to help you and want to give you everything you ever dreamed of. But they will also spend a bit of time criticizing you and chipping away at your self-esteem and self-image as this moves them closer to their goal. While you will notice some of the criticism, you don't think too much about the manipulator trying to harm you. Instead, you feel that they are trying to help you become a better person.

# Chapter 12:
## Favorite Victims

Now, you, like most other people, probably think that you are a pretty steady person. You probably believe that you are not likely to be swayed or taken advantage of too easily. However, most people believe this—most people believe that they are likely to resist manipulation. They don't realize when they do have vulnerabilities, leaving them wide open to exploitation, and manipulators with malicious intent typically can sniff out the reason behind the actions with ease. They can identify those vulnerabilities and take complete advantage of them so easily that you never even realize or suspect it, and that is where they get their power. Manipulators all tend to go for very similar people, and they typically have very predictable vulnerabilities. Let's look at some of the most common:

### EMPATH

The empaths will be individuals who can be deeply sensitive and will discover that they can tune in to others' energy and emotions. They can quickly deal with the feelings of those around them and turn them into their own. This can be a big challenge sometimes if your boundaries aren't that big, because you can absorb the stress and pain of others. However, if you can carefully select the people around you and be careful with your energy, you may find that you attract those with a lot of happiness and joy. You can also absorb these positive emotions in your life.

With dark psychology, your goal is to be able to find people with more positive emotions and use them to your advantage. This doesn't have to be a bad thing. But if you want to get the control and power you want, you may find that you absorb this type of energy at the cost of harming another person. It will take some time to explore this and how it will work later.

Many times, those who use dark psychology like to work with empaths because they can take any negativity, regret and more on their actions and pour it on the other person. An empath will often take on all that guilt and shame without even really knowing why.

The person who made the deed will feel better because they have been able to discharge on the empath, and the empath will suffer.

As an empath, you must first make sure that you have created some healthy limits for yourself. You don't want to go through this process and then find out that someone else is taking advantage of the fact that you are empathetic yourself. But since you already know that the empath you want to work with is an emotional sponge and you can set limits so that it doesn't bounce off you, you will be able to use it to your advantage.

## STRANGERS AND NEW ACQUAINTANCES

As social beings, we always learn and meet new people. But not everyone you meet is authentic. They could make plots to manipulate you in various ways. Meeting new people is severe enough, but adding potential risks further complicates things. Most of the people you meet won't be out to pick you up. Occasionally you may run into a bad actor. Someone with a superficial charm can present themself as a friendly person, but be anything but. Strangers pose a significant risk to your interpersonal relationships. It is, in fact, the opposite scenario: you have nothing to make a psychological profile. In that case, the best solution is to keep your head, but also do your research on who this person is. Closed strangers (closed body posture, a secret about themselves) can be suspicious. On the other hand, they may simply be shy or suffer from social anxiety.

**THE NEED TO PLEASE**

Perhaps the easiest victims of manipulation are those that feel a constant need to please. They are constantly driven forward by this need to make people around them happy. Often, these people are quite naïve; they believe that it is the case that they are only good for making sure that those around them are pleased. Usually, they fear conflict and find that it is vastly easier to give in to conflict and do whatever everyone around them wants than it is to figure out how to avoid the problem entirely.

**THE NEED FOR APPROVAL**

Similarly, some people feel that they must earn the approval of others—they find that they only have any real value when other people believe that they are okay or that other people are accepting them. Their self-esteem is typically drawn entirely from making sure that other people are willing and able to please them, so they find that approval is the only way that they can feel good about themselves.

**THE FEAR OF NEGATIVE EMOTIONS**

When it comes to negative emotions, some people become phobic of them—they are terrified of running into these negative associations with other people and want to do their best to figure out how to avoid triggering negative feelings in other people. They want to make sure that they can avoid being the target of disapproval, frustration or anger, and so they give in to whatever the manipulators request of them in hopes of being able to do better.

## AN INABILITY TO BE ASSERTIVE

Some people are simply known colloquially as doormats—they are too weak to say no to other people, usually for any number of reasons on this list. They may find that they need approval, they are afraid of negativity or any other reason. No matter the reason for their lack of assertiveness, however, they are easy targets for manipulators and are typically favored for that reason.

## WEAK OR NO PERSONAL BOUNDARIES

Similarly, people who struggle with asserting and maintaining their boundaries tend to find that they struggle to protect themselves from manipulation. Boundaries, as you will come to find over time, are perhaps the biggest threats of all time to manipulators. When someone has strong personal boundaries, they can keep themselves separate from the will of other people. They can prevent themselves from falling victim to the ways that people tend to treat them because they will not allow things to get bad enough to let them be victimized in the first place. When those boundaries are missing, however, the manipulator has the perfect storm to simply steamroll over the victim to take control.

## LOW SELF-RELIANCE

Self-reliance is something that everyone needs and yet is so hard to maintain. If you do not feel like you can rely on yourself, there is a good chance that you will find yourself taken advantage of. Feeling like you cannot trust yourself, that you are always wrong when you do something, is perhaps one of the best ways for you to end up the victim of a manipulator at some point.

## A NATURAL NAÏVETÉ

When the target is naturally too naïve to understand what is happening around them or is likely to constantly give the other person the benefit of the doubt, they are going to end up victimized. The common belief behind this is that they would not do something nefarious, so why would anyone else? It is so easy to take advantage of people who always want to see the best in someone else.

## BEING OVERLY CONSCIENTIOUS

Similarly, some people always want to give those around them the benefit of the doubt. When something goes wrong, they assume that it was unintentional. They assume that when someone does something to them, they can justify it somehow, saying that the manipulator probably didn't mean it, or that it was probably an accident. They are so quick to try to see the side of the manipulator that they unintentionally throw themselves under the bus.

## LACKING SELF-CONFIDENCE

People lacking in self-confidence are too quick to let themselves talk themselves out of believing what is happening. They will readily tell themselves that they must have been at fault because they are always at fault. Their beliefs that they can never do anything right typically make them very easy for manipulators to take advantage of.

## SUBMISSIVE PERSONALITY TYPE

Some people have what is known as a submissive personality. They naturally give other people what they want, and they are quick to let themselves depend on other people to make all of the decisions and choose out everything that will happen. They are so dependent upon the other person that they often end up exploited and manipulated, even though they really should have been able to avoid the problem in the first place.

# Chapter 13:

## Body Language

Body language involves how we use our physical behavior, expressions and manners to reveal nonverbal information about ourselves, which is usually done unconsciously. Many people are not aware of it, but in all your interactions, you are constantly giving out body cues and wordless signals that serve either to reinforce the interaction or to contradict what you are trying to say.

Your entire nonverbal behavior transmits a loud and strong message that continues even after you stop talking. There are instances when what someone says might differ from what their body language is communicating. Hence, in this case, it will be easy for the person you are interacting with to pass you off as a liar.

If someone asked for a favor and you gave a smile after giving a no, you have ended up confusing the person. With this kind of mixed signal, the person might be confused about what to believe. However, if the person understands the concept of body language, they would probably just walk away since the body language is unconscious and gives someone away by revealing their true intention.

## THE ESSENCE OF NONVERBAL COMMUNICATION

The cues you are unconsciously giving out from your body are pretty important and, as said earlier, give meaning to the interaction you are in. From your body cues, the person you are with will know whether you are interested in the relationship or not, whether you are hiding information or being plain and whether you are paying attention.

With nonverbal communication signals that complement what you say, you can build trust, rapport and clarity. I am pretty sure you know what happens when your words and body language cues contrast!

In reading body language signals, you have to be keen on noticing the body language people are giving out. It does not stop at that, and you have to be sensitive to yours as well. In understanding nonverbal communication, pay attention to the following roles it plays:

## Repetition

In other words, it enforces the message you are trying to pass. You made a marriage proposal to your girlfriend, for instance. After popping the question and she accepted, you would normally expect her to smile, jump up and be excited. However, if she said yes with a straight face, I am pretty sure you know something is not right.

## Contradiction

It can also refute the message you are passing across, thus giving the signal that you might be lying. You came home from a two-week journey. Your wife greeted you and said she was excited to see you, but without a hug, a smile or any facial expression to corroborate the statement. Something was off.

## Substitution

Body cues often stand in place of verbal communication. In African culture, for instance, let us assume a guest visited a family. As this person was leaving, he offered the child some money. The mother gave the child "that kind of look," and the child took it as a cue to reject the offer.

## Complementing

Body language cues might add more weight to the meaning of the message you are passing across verbally. Consider a man who tells his wife "I love you" and drives off. Another man plants a kiss on the wife's forehead and says "I love you" while looking into her eyes. Of these two, it is clear which one meant what he was saying.

## Accenting

Your nonverbal cues can also emphasize the point you are trying to make. Saying no, alongside a shaking of the head, for instance, emphasizes the weight of the negation.

Without beating around the bush any further, let us examine how you can read various clues from body parts.

### READING VARIOUS PARTS OF THE BODY

## Head Movement

Head movement is one of the simplest body languages to decode. However, for someone who has no clue of what this nonverbal communication signal means, hardly will they be able to make sense of it. To explain head movement, I have here two scenarios:

As part of the exercise to get a job, a candidate is required to make a presentation on why he is the best candidate for the job. During the presentation, his audience, the hiring manager, nods in quick succession while the candidate desperately keeps trying to sell himself. Obviously, he is unaware of the message of the hiring manager, which clearly shows he is wasting his time.

Consider another candidate giving the same presentation. As he goes off trying to sell himself, the hiring manager leans back with his head tilted. Oblivious to the meaning of this body language, the candidate does not try to shed light on the point that triggered the manager's body reaction. He is ignorant of the body language; hence, he keeps on blabbing.

Below are some common head movement signals and their meanings:

When a person gives quick, successive nods, they are probably fed up with the interaction. Had the candidate in our first example known this, he would have tried harder to impress the manager or end the interaction, saving him time.

A slow nod is a sure sign of interest in the interaction. This is what the candidate should be after, had he any knowledge of nonverbal communication and body language. It is also the same when the person you are with tilts their head sideways.

A slight, backward tilt of the head is a sign of suspicion, uncertainty or confusion. This, at times, might be accompanied by a slight change in facial expression. This is a cue to clarify the last point that triggered such an expression. The candidate in our second example could have cashed in on this point and clarified his statement.

If you are having a discussion with a group of people and one of them starts scratching their jaw, there is a big chance that the person is not in agreement with the subject of discussion. Be sure to allow the person to voice out their view.

## Reading the Face

There are many expressions we can reveal with our face. Even babies and toddlers are smart enough to decode this body language cue. A smile reveals happiness or satisfaction. A frown shows dissatisfaction or sadness. There are times as well when the facial expression could give insight into what is really going on with a person. A person who says they're fine with a slight frown, for instance, could be lying.

It is a universal form of expression that conveys a wide range of emotions, such as sadness, fear, panic, anxiety, worry, disgust, distrust, happiness and many others. The best part is that this expression does not change or vary with people.

Many people, in a bid to hide their true intention, desperately try to control the face. A careful study of the face, however, can give you a clear glimpse into the message someone is trying to pass across. There are times when someone might hide obvious body language, such as raised eyebrows, smiles, frowns, etc. Be sure to watch out for the following:

A warm and genuine smile does light up the whole face. It indicates happiness. It is also a sure indication that the other party is enjoying your company.

A fake smile, on the other hand, is a polite way of showing approval, even if the person does not enjoy the conversation or interaction. For you to detect a fake smile, take a look at the side of the eyes. The lack of crinkles is all you need to pass a smile off as fake.

## The Eye Window

The eyes reveal a lot about a person. This explains why the eyes are referred to as the window to the soul. Besides, in all forms of interactions, it is an important and natural communication process for you to take note of the eyes.

In communicating with people, it is normal to take note of eye contact, whether someone is averting your gaze or not, the rate of blinking, and the size of their pupils.

The following explains some nonverbal clues from the eyes:

### Eye gaze

A person interested and paying attention to a conversation will look directly into your eyes while having a conversation, although they might break eye contact once in a while because prolonged eye contact is rather uncomfortable. A distracted and uninterested person, on the other hand, will often break eye contact and look away. This person might be uncomfortable or is trying to hide their true feelings.

### Blinking

While blinking is a completely natural process, the frequency matters. A person uncomfortable or in distress will blink more often. Infrequent blinking, on the other hand, means that a person is intentionally trying to control their eye movements.

## Pupil size

Pay attention to the pupil size as it is very subtle and is affected by the level of light in the room. However, emotions also do affect pupil dilation, as it can cause small changes in the size of the pupil. This explains why someone with highly dilated eyes is either aroused or interested in a person.

## Hand Movements

There are some cues that can easily be found from the position and pattern of movement of the hand. We explain this in detail:

When someone has their hands in their pockets, they could be lacking confidence, hiding information, or just being defensive.

In a group or meeting, when a person unconsciously points to another person while making a speech, there might be some common ground they share.

In communicating with someone, the presence of an obstacle in the form of an object between you and the person translates to the person trying to block you out. In this case, your aim should be to build rapport and gain the trust of such a person.

A person talking with the palms facing up is likely being honest. Such a person is not hiding the palm since they most likely have nothing to hide.

# **The Mouth**

The expressions and movement of the mouth are pretty vital in decoding body language as well. This is why a person who is worried, anxious or insecure will likely chew their lower lip. Some forms of nonverbal communication cues from the mouth will be examined below. A person, in an effort to be polite, might cover the mouth if the other party is yawning. Be watchful, as it can be done to cover up a frown as well.

## *Pursed lips*

When a person tightens up their lip, it could signal objection, disapproval or distaste.

## *Lip biting*

This is common when a person is anxious, worried or stressed.

## *Covering the mouth*

This could be done in an effort to hide emotional reactions like smiles or smirks.

## *A slight change in direction*

A person's feelings can be seen through the direction of the mouth. As a result, someone happy or in a good mood might have their mouth slightly turned up. A slightly turned-down mouth, on the other hand, could signal sadness or displeasure.

# THE IMPORTANCE OF READING PEOPLE

The world is made of people. Life is better enjoyed when you have people to relate with. However, your survival in the world also depends on your ability to decide when not to cooperate with some people, and that is why your ability to read people is important.

There are times you are unconsciously cooperating with others. The fact that you walk gently to your place of work without causing a scene or doing anything to warrant unnecessary attention is an act of cooperation with the rest of the society on some level. You don't just wake up one day and decide to go on a killing spree. You are connected to the Internet and the rest of the world alike. All these things require some form of human cooperation.

For this to take place, people unconsciously have to come to a reasonable form of agreement and acceptable behavior on some level. All in all, cooperating with people is pretty important, and your decision whether to cooperate or not comes down to your ability to read people.

The best salesman knows how to coax you because they are good at analyzing people. They can get you into buying what they have to offer even if you do not need what they are offering. The better you are at reading other people's motives, the better you can deal with such a person.

As established above, the ability to read people is inherent in everyone. In all your day-to-day interactions with people, the following takes place:

## <u>You consciously judge them</u>

In other words, you assess the way they dress, the way they look and their overall appearance. You try to understand their motives and behaviors.

## <u>You consciously read them</u>

In other words, you judge their body language and think about their appearance. This happens to anyone you are interacting with. You consciously examine a couple of things about them.

## <u>You give an appropriate response based on your assessment</u>

This is after the first two steps above and just in the first minute of interaction.

Throughout the conversation or interaction, you evaluate the person consciously. This is the basic in which all forms of human interaction take place.

### LEARN TO DECODE BODY LANGUAGE

Consider their pose. Is it strong and confident, or is it shy and timid? A person adopting a dominant posture, like the arms akimbo, for instance, and taking a lot of space is probably the one in charge.

Consider eye contact while having a conversation. Do they give forth intense eye contact? Do they blink too much? Are they avoiding your gaze? Avoiding your gaze could suggest hiding information or distrust.

Do they put forward an open body language? For instance, are the arms and legs crossed or opened? This suggests an interest in the interaction. The opposite, on the other hand, means a lack of interest in the conversation.

Check the direction of their feet. If it is pointed toward you, they probably want to talk to you. If it is pointed away, probably toward the door, they want to leave.

Know some subtle signs of attraction a woman will give you. She could have her feet or back pointed directly at you. She could be adjusting her clothes, twirling her hair or improving her appearance in a certain way.

Someone touching themselves is probably uncomfortable and needs to feel calm. They might be uncomfortable because of the subject of conversation, environment or person. Touch makes people feel better by releasing endorphins.

Check if they are fidgety or too still. Excess stillness is a classic sign of distrust. If someone is free with you and trusts you, they will likely move their body parts freely. On the other hand, if they are too anxious or nervous, they could fidget a lot.

There will be many more on decoding body language in a later chapter.

All in all, try to be aware of the overall energy someone is giving off in the interaction. This is natural with humans, and if you feel closed off from the person's body language, listen to your intuition. The person probably does not want you around.

Also, in decoding body language, take note of micro-expressions. These are expressions evident in someone's face. However, either they are not aware of them or they try so hard to hide them. Micro-expressions are common when you are with someone you are not so sure of.

This is common when you first meet someone, and the skepticism is evident. It could also happen when there is a shift in the relationship — for instance, finding out a dirty secret about someone, making you distrust them.

As evident from the above examples, micro-expressions occur when there is tension. They happen when the parties involved make eye contact. For instance, a broad smile could suddenly become a frown for a fraction of a second.

In reading someone's body language, it is essential to take note of the person's behavior in context. In other words, is the behavior of the person appropriate in the situation? What does their dress infer? Is something peculiar about their clothing or overall appearance?

Body language occurs in a cluster; in other words, a particular body language needs to correspond with the entire picture.

It is also essential to know that people can fake their body language. It could be an innocent act or a ploy to deceive you. People could go out of their way to be nice to you if they want something from you. To build rapport, for instance, they could mimic your body language.

# Chapter 14:
## Secrets to Protect Yourself

## KEEP A JOURNAL OF YOUR CONVERSATIONS

There are usually some types of signs which send hints that someone is trying to manipulate you. Of course, these are not always easy to spot, unless you have been in the situation before or understand manipulation.

One strategy you can do if you feel that someone is manipulating you is to keep a journal of what is said. You can write down your conversations or things they randomly say to you. At the same time, you can also write down what they do.

While this might seem like an unconventional thing to do, it can help you observe what is truly going on because manipulators work on an emotional level. This is often hard to spot, especially if you already lack confidence in yourself.

You can also include how the situation or words stated made you feel. You might find a connection between what the manipulator states and how you feel. For example, you might find that your self-image is starting to decrease. When you notice this, it is a sign that you need to stay away from the person or get out of the relationship as quickly as possible.

## CONFRONT MANIPULATORS ABOUT THEIR BEHAVIOR

This is going to be easier with some people than others. For example, if the manipulator is your supervisor and you need your job, you might not directly confront them. You also might struggle to confront your significant other, especially if they have lowered your self-esteem. However, confronting the manipulator is a great way to let them know you understand their behavior and you will not stand for it.

If you take this approach, you want to be aware of the other strategies they could use against you. For instance, they might try to create a distraction or try to play the victim. They also might blame someone else for their behavior or tell you that you are imagining everything.

When you confront a manipulator, you need to be firm. You need to be completely convinced and understand that they will try to manipulate you as they don't want other people to catch on to their behavior. You also need to be cautious because some manipulators can get passive aggressive or violent.

## HAVE THE RIGHT MINDSET

Another way to eliminate a manipulator from your life is to have a strong mindset. You want to make sure that you feel confident in your abilities to stop them from using techniques against you. You also want to make sure your self-esteem and self-image is positive. At the same time, you want to understand the ways they will manipulate you.

You need to understand their techniques in order to combat them. You need to understand that they probably won't stop with just one technique. They will more than likely use a few in hopes that they can start to break you down.

The more you remain strong, the more likely the manipulator will leave you alone. Manipulators won't spend a lot of time trying to use different techniques if you continuously push them away, call them out on their behavior and continue to believe in yourself.

## MEDITATE

Many people don't realize how much meditation can help. Meditation is not only meant to keep you calm, but it also works to keep you positive and feeling good about yourself. When you feel this way, you will find it easier to eliminate the negativity from your life, which means manipulators.

Meditation is basic and you don't need to put aside a lot of time. You can schedule about ten minutes out of your day for meditation. Find a time and place where you can be alone and uninterrupted. You also want it to be quiet so you can concentrate on eliminating the negativity from your body and mind.

Many people will use breathing techniques to help them remain focused during meditation. This is when you close your eyes and start breathing normally. You want to focus on your breath. Notice how your clothes feel on your body or place one hand on your chest and your other hand on your stomach. Feel how your hands move as you breathe in and out. You will then focus on deep breaths. Take a deep breath in and then exhale slowly. Complete this exercise until you feel calm.

Meditation will not only help you eliminate manipulators who haven't become a close person in your life, but it will also help you manage your life with a manipulator. Of course, you want to leave if your significant other is a manipulator for your own mental health and safety, but meditation can help give you strength. It can give you the strength to focus on your mindset and find ways to protect yourself from the manipulative techniques. It can also give you the strength to leave, once you are ready.

## BEGIN WITH BUILDING A SUPPORT NETWORK

It is vital that you have support from friends and family. This can be a difficult one though. It could be that the very partner you have just left browbeat you to severing all personal ties. If this is your situation and you are unable to pick up those ties, then there are organizations that you can turn to. These agencies can guide you in dealing with your situation.

It is going to be a rough ride and you may even need a safe house where your partner does not know where to find you. Don't feel ashamed. If you have children it will be even harder, but for their sakes, get them away. They can make contact again in later years if they so wish. Then they may better understand what happened. Bear this in mind that if you feel stifled, then almost certainly they do too.

That is, of course, the worst scenario. No matter how hard it is for you to leave, you must take the time for yourself, and recoup.

The easiest targets are those who are already isolated or are easy to isolate. By surrounding yourself with a network of friends, family and even a support group that pertains to the victims of manipulators could do wonders in terms of protecting you in the future. The more people around you, the more roadblocks the manipulator sees to get you under control.

## BUILD UP YOUR COURAGE

Once you have built up your courage and self-esteem, you can face the world head-on. We all approach this one in a different way. The first rule must be not to compare yourself to others. It is not an easy rule to follow, but nonetheless, you are new to freedom. That is exactly what you are, free. Forget other people. Of course, be polite, but concentrate on your needs and not anyone else's, unless you have children.

There will come a time when you must begin to take risks. That is after the huge risk you have put yourself through by leaving. You have taken a huge leap forward, no need to jump in feet first, give it time to settle.

A great exercise for those who are worriers, is to write down all the worst situations you feel may befall you. Once you have a thorough list, the next stage is to consider how you might deal with each of them. Take notes on your best plan and strategy. This will show you the problem from a detached perspective. It will help you determine which approach is best for each situation. If you feel it is too overwhelming, then break it down into smaller and more manageable steps. As you tackle each micro-step, before you know it, you will have reached the last one. Baby steps do lead to resolving the whole problem.

You will make mistakes! The proverb, "To err is human," is true. You need to embrace any mistakes you make and learn from them.

Learning the right way to do something is so much easier when you have knowledge of the wrong way. You're not perfect, no one is, but you only need to be as perfect as you yourself want to be.

## BECOME SELF-AWARE

Self-awareness is based on your ability to discern your strengths and weaknesses and identify your emotions. It entails getting cognizant of your unique and natural personality, helping to narrow in on recognizing the beliefs, motivations and thoughts that determine your daily activities. It equips you with the ability to appreciate others, fathom their perceptions in your direction and understand your true mentality and reactions towards them. Self-recognition is a principal source of your strong character; it strengthens who you are at your core. Becoming self-aware makes it easier to be authentic, trustworthy and able to express your accurate self without regret. By understanding yourself better, guess what happens - you want help from other people in group efforts in order to supplement your own deficits. Additionally, a strong sense of self-awareness helps to lead a business with purpose and utmost transparency.

Self-awareness is such a crucial step in emotional cleverness because you must know yourself and any predicament in your life before you even fathom as to why you (or other people) feel certain feelings. To attain this point, you need to dive within the self and reflect on your life knowledge with an open mind.

## PRACTICE SELF-CARE

Taking good care of your individual needs through things like relaxation, eating healthy and exercise can be important. Although EQ demands you to empathize with others, it does not in any way imply that you must do so at the expense of your wellbeing. In fact, if you don't take good care of yourself, you'll probably only execute a mediocre job at caring for anyone else and if you manage this, you will burn out quickly. Taking care of yourself will ultimately provide you with the capacity and strength to take care of others.

The manipulator will look for people who do not value themselves. Those who do not see their own inherent value are typically much easier at manipulating into doing what they desire simply because they do not think they deserve better, and when they feel like they do not deserve better, they are not likely to resist the manipulation, even when it hurts them. By focusing on self-care, you are telling yourself that you are valuable. You are giving yourself the care you deserve to ensure that you are healthy and cared for, which makes you less desirable. While most people will find confidence attractive, the manipulator wants nothing to do with it.

## DEVELOP SELF-ESTEEM

This might be easier said than done, but it is still relevant — you should always seek out ways to develop your own self-esteem. When you do, you will find that you are a much happier and healthier individual. That alone will make you less attractive to the manipulator for the same reasons that focusing on self-care will make you less attractive.

## LOWER YOUR STRESS LEVELS GREATLY

Stress may greatly stand in the way of you managing your emotions effortlessly, especially because it inhibits emotional intelligence by causing you to react on impulse or irrationally. Therefore, you ought to find ways of de-stressing if you wish to have any strength to regulate your emotions. Be creative at overcoming stress, for instance through positive affirmations, overcoming procrastination, waking up early to beat visitors, having a gratitude list, meditation, etc.

The people you surround yourself with will greatly influence whether you are capable of controlling your emotions or not. If you surround yourself with psychological wrecks for instance, they will probably infect you with similar character traits. Therefore, evaluate the actions and terms that those you spend time with screen and decide whether this is the kind of lifestyle you desire for yourself. For instance, people who put you down, always complaining and being negative, could turn you into one of them easily. This greatly decreases the likelihood of taking charge of your emotions when around them. The point is to not let people impact your emotions and the ones who you spend the most time with have an increased chance of doing this. The relationships you have must be mutually beneficial emotionally. It is much harder to practice emotional stability if you are around emotional leeches on a regular basis. After having gained an improved understanding of yourself, it is important to know how to regulate and manage yourself.

## MANAGE YOUR FEELINGS

After gaining self-awareness and connecting with your true self, you must develop the ability to make sure that everything you have discovered thus far works for your benefit. This ability is what connects emotional intelligence with self-management.

EQ self-regulation or self-management involves governing your feelings. With self-management, you are able to gain total control over your reactions. The goal with this is to be able to have positive emotions towards all circumstances. Self-management will not totally eliminate your feelings of anger; nonetheless, it does provide you with the ability to control and learn to convert it into positive energy. You may use this energy to seek solutions to situations that would generally cause anger.

So how exactly do you put the feelings you've identified, as well as any kind of emotions that may unexpectedly arise under your whole control? It may look like a lot to handle, but through the advancement of self-regulation abilities you will find it to become sort of a secondary character. EQ self-management comprises many facets, such as stress administration, intentionality, integrity, achievement travel, emotional self-control, being proactive genuinely, taking positive initiative and versatility, among numerous others. All these tenets help you realize and cope with potential behavioral complications before they get out of hands and degenerate into devastating consequences.

**DEVELOPING EMOTIONAL SELF-CONTROL**

Before diving into this area of the guide, it is important to learn that both positive and negative emotions can take control over you. Don't be fooled by the positive emotions that seem enjoyable as they envelop you. Normally, as they can bring you to new heights, you could just as easily be brought crashing down if they're not controlled. They can lead you astray and make you lie to yourself about particular things since they make you feel great. So, both positive and negative emotions work against you when you allow them to take control. It is therefore essential to master emotions of all kinds so that you can take complete charge of your life; not allowing yourself to react with techniques that are detrimental to yourself and to others.

## DON'T FALL INTO THEIR TRAP

Most of us come across instances where others seek to manipulate our thoughts, attitudes or actions and take advantage of them to their own advantage. In one such case, you fail to understand the true motive. The person mentally dominates you, and you step into the pit. Often this emotional abuse costs you a lot when you make some critical decisions under another person's control, and you know it later, when it is too late.

You have to be conscious when a relationship sounds too good to be true. They are showering you with compassion, gratitude, admiration, congratulations, and affection. You feel like you live in a dream where everything seems perfect. They don't give you a reason to worry. You simply cannot find any flaws in them. Also, if anything goes wrong, they can begin to weep or feel sorry. You have become the object of extreme intimacy and have the feeling of passion for a fairy tale.

It is the outcome because you actually began the relationship with love bombing and all of a sudden, you start feeling ignored. You are receiving gratitude, presents and recognition, but rarely. You feel like you're losing your hold or having someone else in your life. You get another gift from them the moment you make up your mind to move on. You find it hard to make up your own mind. They are trying to get leverage over you in one situation like this. For most instances, this works to your amazement. You approach them much more.

Individuals often succeed in manipulating their victims after intermittent reinforcement. We can avoid behaving in the same way while fighting back or demanding an answer. The explanation is that they are really taking complete care of you now, so they say goodbye to the intermittent strengthening. We no longer really need it. Manipulators have many different faces, and in the same manner, they can use many different ways to get things done. The person may make an undertaking, and later deny that you begin to doubt your own perception. They make you feel bad when you try hard to make them aware of their promise. They can employ shallow sympathy and burst into crocodile tears. Eventually, you end up trusting them and even doubting whether you listened correctly.

You can't believe smiling faces that seem confident and strong. Manipulative people often have self-serving prejudice, so they think less for the other person's feelings. We have a reason to look for others who affirm them and make them even feel superior.

## STEER STRAIGHT WHEREVER POSSIBLE

There are some circumstances in which you can't fully leave a relationship-most, usually whether that person is a parent or an extended family member. You probably cannot go cold turkey unless the individual causes serious harm or psychological damage. Next, you need to accept this person completely for who they are and change your relationship standards accordingly. If they were someone you needed validation from before, then you would have to quit looking for their validation. Recognize that their advice is not something you need in your life if they were someone you received advice from. When they keep offering it, you can thank them for it, and then politely dump it. When setting these limits, be as discreet as you can, and do not tell the other person you are setting them. Creating this shift at your end will take some time, and when you get upset with the other person in the process, you will have to deal with their reaction on top of that.

Knowing this will drain your energy a little bit, setting limits around the time you spend with that person. If you've been hanging out every Saturday with your manipulating mother-in-law, cut it down to once a month and plan something for that day so that there is a definite end time for your hangout.

## CALL THEM OUT ON THEIR ACTIONS

Manipulators are always difficult to deal with, but the worst are discreet manipulators. They will stay cool as a cucumber and yet rigid and unbending when confronted. You may start to get frustrated when you start seeing their faulty reasoning. When you keep fighting with them, you'll find it hard not to raise your voice a bit. You're going to start looking like the irrational one, and they're going to try to take back control by remaining calm, based on their "maturity."

Defending yourself is tempting and trying to get the other person to see what is really going on. But a true manipulator will not change their tune, and the more you give in to that urge to protect yourself, the more they will twist your words. It will not be long before you get stuck in this twisted web of myths and false expectations. If you are in a situation with a true manipulator, the two goals for any conflict that is taking place should be to resolve and leave, whether that means leaving the current conversation or exiting the relationship. Evade threats, accusations, losing patience, accusing the other person of coercion or becoming excessively emotional. Stick to honest, factual and respectful declarations when you speak.

There are things that require a high degree of intelligence, flexibility and self-discipline when dealing with a manipulative person. You might not have the self-control to react without losing your temper and making things worse. If that's the case, accept this about yourself and take extra steps to avoid a tense confrontation (invite a mediator into the conversation, for example, or send an email instead of meeting in person, so you have time to think through what you say).

For me, it can cause a bit of tension to deal with someone who loses their temper. I needed to have a friend with me in order to feel secure in circumstances where there were a lot of blow-up risks. Much as I wished I could handle the conflict myself, I realized that I wasn't quite in a position to do so. I would have felt a lot of needless discomfort if I had failed to acknowledge this about myself because of my decision to act better than I was. Wouldn't you be better at handling the problem than you are? Others will be attacking the vulnerable points and trying to make it seem like the problem will be easier for you to deal with than it is. Do not equate your reaction to someone else's reaction in one case.

**IGNORE WHAT THEY DO AND SAY**

It is intended to ignore the dishonest people. These people flip flop over things, they're slippery when you try to keep them accountable, they promise support that never comes, they 're always making you feel guilty - everything you don't want in a person. The greatest mistake you can make when dealing with a dishonest person is trying to correct them. You sink deeper into their pit by correcting them. Humans will use anger and misunderstanding to lure you into a confrontation. We want to make you feel nervous so that they can see how you tick. When they learn the triggering factors, you are going to use them to affect your actions. A smarter approach is to ignore them entirely. Only erase them from your life if you can't delete them instantly-even if they're a supervisor, coworker or member of the family who agree with what they're doing and then carry on doing your own thing anyway.

## TOUCH THEIR CENTRE OF GRAVITY

Manipulative people actively take advantage of their own tactics against you. Through your enemies, they will become enemies, and turn them against you. They're going to dangle some small reward in front of you and make you chase it relentlessly - they're going to take it away any time you get close to it. You will forever keep past acts above your head. And so on and so forth. Avoid letting those who exploit you use their tactics against you. Turn the tables on them instead. Build your own plan and hit them where it hurts. When you are forced to deal with a dishonest person who, no matter how hard you try to avoid them, tries to make your life miserable, you have only one choice - find their center of gravity and destroy it. This center may be associates, followers or subordinates to the deceptive individual. It may be a high-level talent or advanced knowledge of a particular area. They can manage it as a particular resource.

Figure out what their center of gravity is and make it yours anyway. Create alliances with those close to them, hire people to replace them with their skill sets and knowledge base, or siphon away their precious assets. This will throw them off balance and push them to concentrate on managing their life, not yours.

## BELIEVE IN YOUR DECISION

You know better than anyone else what is best for your future. So many people are going around asking for the views of other people on anything. What do I want to do with my life? What am I fantastic at? Where am I, then? Avoid searching for other people so you can describe yourself. Define yourself. Believe in yourself. What distinguishes winners from losers is not the ability to listen to other people's opinions; it's the ability to listen to one's own opinions. You prevent dishonest people from influencing your life by setting up your own values and sticking to them tightly. This will serve as a firewall to your convictions, keeping manipulators ostracized and out of your way.

## TRY NOT TO FIT RIGHT IN

Keep reinventing yourself. One myth is the belief that continuity is somehow admirable or related to achievement. Manipulative people want you to be consistent so that they can count on you to advance their agendas. They want you to show up at 9 am every day and work at minimum wage for them. They want you to come home on time and make them feel good about themselves and clean the house.

## CONSISTENT ASSEMBLY LINES

The prison is uniform. Consistency is how they trap you in a shell. It's their way of manipulating you. The only way to stop being exploited is by consciously going against all the barriers other people seek to create for you. Hold on trying to blend in. Instead, look to stand out. Act to be different in some way, and never remain the same for too long. By design, personal growth needs a lack of consistency. Constant change is expected - constant reinvention.

## AVOID CONCESSION

Guilt is an emotion to no use. But it is a powerful tool. Guilt is one of those weapons that would be used against you by dishonest people. They will make you feel bad for past defeats and small mistakes, or they will make you feel guilty for being overconfident and prideful. They'll use it against you if you feel happy or sure of yourself. One can ever feel too good about themselves; they will claim. Another tool that is being used against you by manipulators is doubt. They will work to instill within you a sense of self-doubt about your ability and your worth. Their ultimate goal is to take you off balance and make you put yourself in second place. Within this state of confusion, manipulators gain control. Their power is getting greater and it becomes twice as likely to convince you to compromise on your principles, ambitions and yourself.

Simple solution - avoid feeling guilty. Avoid asking yourself. When it comes to your own life, you owe nothing to no-one. You deserve to feel good about yourself and to be stunned by your achievements. You deserve to have a good sense of confidence and self-belief in what you do. It is neither moral nor enlightened to compromise on either of these issues. This is then the path to self-destruction.

## NEVER ASK FOR PERMISSION

Asking for forgiveness is better than asking for permission. The problem is that we have been conditioned to ask for permission constantly. As children, we had to ask for everything we wanted — to be fed, changed and burped. We had to ask permission to go to the bathroom every day, and we had to wait to eat lunch at a designated time and wait for our turn to play with toys. As a result, most people never cease to expect permission.

Employees around the world are waiting for a promotion and waiting for their turn to talk. Most are so used to being chosen that they sit in meetings in silence, afraid to talk out of turn or even lift their hands. It's a different way of living.

What if you did it whenever you wanted to do it? And if you quit being too worried about politeness and feeling relaxed with others? What if, instead, you lived your life exactly the way you wanted to? They are all things you can do whenever you want.

Manipulative people want you to feel constrained by some abstract law or principle that says you can't behave freely without consulting an authority figure or a party. The reality is that at any given moment, you can miss this feeling of confinement. You will continue living a completely different life today than you did yesterday. The decision is yours.

## BUILD A GREATER SENSE OF MISSION

Destiny driven people aren't easily fooled. The reason manipulators in this world tend to prosper is that so many people lead a purposeless life. If there is no reason in your life, you cannot believe something. They're going to do anything. Because nothing matters, somehow. People who lack intent literally waste time. There is no rhyme or explanation for the manner in which they live their lives. They don't know where to go or why they are here. So, to avoid going insane, they work meaningless jobs and stuff their minds full of celebrity gossip, reality television and other useless types of media. They remain busy to avoid the desperate feeling of emptiness growing inside them. This profession and loneliness empower deceptive individuals.

Every minute, a sucker is born. When you are constantly distracted, constantly consuming pointless content, trying to stay constantly busy – you are the sucker. By peddling meaningless knowledge and events to them, manipulators manipulate purposeless people. The only way to escape that scenario is by cultivating a sense of destiny. Destiny is doing away with distraction. The manipulators can't hurt you because you think about where you're going. They cannot confuse you or lead you astray.

## TAKE NEW OPPORTUNITIES

The universe wants to put your eggs in one bowl. People all around you ask you to lock yourself in a mortgage, a car payment, a secure relationship, a single position at the office. They want you staked down to a single chance for the rest of your life. Nowadays, it is also looked down on being optimistic. Staying hungry is also seen as a sign of weakness. How can't you just be happy with what you have? Why should you be so greedy? If you show a desire for more, this is what dishonest people would ask you. They're going to call you vain, greedy or prideful. They'll make you feel cold and uncomfortable like you're heartless and inhumane. The reality is that they want to keep you in your place. They want you to stay at the same job and spend the rest of your life living in the same place. They want you and the structures they control to remain dependent upon them.

The only way to stay autonomous is to look for new possibilities and build new ones actively. Continue applying for new jobs, starting new companies, developing new partnerships and seeking new experiences.

## AVOID BEING AN INFANT

When you get fooled by someone, shame on them. When you're fooled by someone ten times, you're an idiot. Avoid making manipulators walk all over you from being a snap pack. Nobody feels sorry for you, and you're always being humiliated. Have enough self-consciousness and reverence for yourself to say no to dishonest people.

You cannot just walk around life blaming the troubles on others. You cannot simply walk away from the people trying to control you through life either. Yes, there are people who are negative and manipulative. And yes, these people are going to try to use you. Yet that doesn't mean that you have a free pass to make mistakes and exploit them. Without your permission, no-one can control you. You are to blame for your own achievements and defeats. If others outstrip you, it's your fault, not theirs, be smart. Learn from your mistakes. Don't believe the same slippery person again and again. Cut them off. Remove them from your life. Commit to connecting yourself with like-minded people who will not be exploiting you.

**BETTING ON YOURSELF**

Take a gamble on the one thing in life that you can control - yourself. Too many people restrict themselves to considering only external factors when making difficult decisions. They consider the financial consequences of a situation and its relationships. Yet they fail to acknowledge the impact on their personal satisfaction and sense of self-worth that their choice would have. As a result, when they should be taking chances on themselves, they take chances on other people. Then, they wonder why they are sad.

If you just take chances on strangers and things, you put yourself at the mercy of those people and stuff. It makes you weak and ready to exploit. You should take chances on yourself instead. In any tough situation you find yourself facing, don't ask questions like, "Who's the right one to side with?" or "What choice would be more likely to succeed?" Rather say, "What am I most likely to do?" So go out and do that. For example, if you have an opportunity to start your own company or keep working at the same dead-end job, don't keep in the job only because the pay is just slightly pathetic. Don't just live, because the relationships are slightly unpleasant. You are betting on external factors when you do so. This is also a mistake. Betting on yourself is a safer plan.

You will never regret making a bet on yourself. You will, of course, have to take full responsibility for any mistakes that you make. Sure, you need to stick to a higher standard. Yet you too must be solely responsible for your own victories. You will continue to rise and achieve greater and higher rates of success.

**STOP GETTING EMOTIONALLY ATTACHED TO THEM**

All you do with a manipulator is false. Every fight you have been going through is your fault. Manipulating will wreak havoc on your feelings. You go from crying to being furious to in the short term feeling guilty and indignant. Then you are sorry you have not stuck up for yourself. You are ashamed to let them get started again on you. Your emotions are more stable once you've left a manipulator.

Life is a journey into an adventure. On the way, many people come to keep us company at various points for a certain amount of time and go after they play their part in our lives. There is no problem with the persons coming and going themselves, but the difficulties occur when you are emotionally attached to the persons and feel powerless, tense and worried when the relationship ends with an emotional manipulator particularly. Therefore, if you want to stay healthy and make progress in life, you need to resolve the emotional connection as soon as possible. There is no doubt that some individuals will become the driving force for you to move towards the path chosen. But being separated from them, you should be careful not to get distracted. You need to make judicious use of the relationships. Be attached to individuals with a detached approach and take care of them to create a confident atmosphere. However, when you let them go out of your life for being a manipulator because some other relationship is waiting on your journey, you should not be dependent on that person for your growth and stop your life. You need to re-focus on your journey, which leaves past memories behind.

Handling emotional connection measures the degree of sophistication of one's journey down the desired direction and its gravity. Treat yourself to a moment you share with friends. Learn from them, love them and look after them, but don't make them walking sticks. Much of the time, people are usually afraid to lose someone because of their incapacity to go on in life alone. So, if you dare walk alone on the chosen path, you no longer have to conquer the emotional connection.

## TELL THEM "YOU'RE OK."

This begins with the way you used to not respond to their techniques anymore. If you don't want to, you say "no," or you speak your mind even though they don't like it. Work on feeling ok with how negatively they may react. When they're not yours, don't pick them up.

You can only keep your actions under control. That's crucial because you won't be able to alter a manipulator's behavior; however, you can avoid being their victim. That happens when you start saying "No." The first step in breaking the cycle is realize we are manipulated because we allow it and to refuse to be manipulated. Manipulators are good at what they do, so watch out for their reaction. They will probably say or do things that tug at the heartstrings. We will stand firm in our "no," realizing we are taking the first step to free ourselves from its power.

## LET GO OF NASTY RELATIONSHIPS

Toxic partnerships can be hard to let go of. Many people find themselves caught in a cycle of returning to relationships that are not good for them. This just creates a cycle of hurt and grief. Toxic relationships can be let go of there. Psychologists have worked with people who have had enough of this issue to be able to write a whole handbook about it. The very first step to getting out of a toxic relationship is admitting to yourself that the relationship isn't perfect. You might note and try to explain the signs of a toxic relationship with yourself. It's called "cognitive dissonance" if you notice that uncomfortable feeling in the back of your mind, and it's your brain trying to protect you from what you know is true. Take note of the things that make you feel this way in a relationship. The first step is to recognize that your connection is toxic. You have to be conscious of all the things that affect you before you can truly be free.

Relationships are a side lane. Two people are involved in the relationship, meaning that two people are involved in all the disagreements, arguments and behavior. You cannot fully take the blame onto yourself. If you blame yourself for all of the relationship problems, you'll find yourself going back to trying to fix them. Recognize that both parties are sometimes at fault for a dysfunctional relationship. Recognize your responsibilities - but your responsibilities alone. Within a toxic relationship, you don't need to be up to anyone else's issues. There's no need to hoist it on yourself because you aren't to blame.

Listing your emotions is just part of the fight — you need skills to control your emotions as well. Think of your current abilities to cope. Should you eat something when you're nervous? Should you drink to keep yourself calm? When you're mad, will you tell your friends? If you're anxious, will you stay home? These conventional strategies can make you feel better right now, but they will make you feel worse in the long run. Search for long-term coping strategies that are perfect for you. Keep in mind that what works for one person doesn't always work for another, and you need to figure out what's best for you to manage your emotions. Experimenting with various coping mechanisms to figure out what works for you - deep breathing, exercising, meditating, reading, painting and spending time in nature are only a few of the techniques that could help.

The way you think has an impact on how you feel and how you behave. You are deprived of intellectual energy by saying things like, "I can't take this," or "I'm such an idiot." Pay attention to what you think. You'll probably note rising trends and themes. Maybe you're telling yourself about things you feel uncomfortable about doing. Or maybe you're telling yourself you're not in control of your life.

Respond with something more constructive to the unproductive and unreasonable feelings. But instead of saying, "I 'm going to screw this up," think, "This is my chance to shine, and I'm going to do my best." Changing the interactions you're having with yourself can be the most instrumental thing you can do to improve your existence. Changing your attitude is the only way to teach your brain to think differently. Do tough things — and keep doing them even though you don't think you should. You will be demonstrating to yourself that you are stronger than you think. Set up healthy daily habits too. Practice appreciation, exercise, get plenty of sleep and follow a balanced diet in order for the brain and body to be at its best. Seek out individuals who inspire you to be your best. And create an atmosphere that helps you develop a balanced lifestyle.

Many of the world's positive habits won't work if you practice them alongside your bad habits. It is like eating donuts on a treadmill while you're running. Pay attention to your bad habits (we all have them) that rob you of your mental strength. Whether you feel bad for yourself or envy the success of other people, it takes only one or two to keep you stuck in life. Once you realize your bad habits, spend energy replacing them with healthier alternatives. You will then be able to step out of the hamster wheel and actively work towards your goals.

Just as it takes time and practice to become physically strong, so too, it takes dedication to build mental strength. But the key to feeling your best and reaching your most significant potential is to build mental muscle.

**GIVE YOURSELF CONSTRUCTIVE SELF-APPRAISAL ALL DAY LONG**

An emotional manipulator will completely tarnish your mood, so make sure you restore yourself during the day with uplifting self-talks. Each of us has a set of messages that keep playing in our minds over and over. Our responses to life and its circumstances are represented by this internal dialog or personal commentary. One way to recognize, encourage and maintain optimism, hope and happiness is to fill our minds with optimistic self-talking consciously. Far too often, because of our manipulative partner, the self-talk pattern that we have formed is negative. They recall the derogatory things our friends, parents, siblings or teachers told us as children. We remember other children's adverse reactions, which undermined the way we felt about ourselves. Such messages have been playing in our minds over the years, strengthening our feelings of rage, fear, guilt and hopelessness.

Some of the most important approaches used in dealing with those suffering from depression are to determine the root of these messages and to work with the individual to "overwrite" them deliberately. If a person learned they were worthless as a child, we'd show them how special they really are. If a person has learned to expect disasters and catastrophic events while growing up, we will teach them a better way to predict the future.

Check the exercise below. Within your head, write down some of the negative thoughts that hinder your desire to resolve your circumstances. Whenever possible, be precise and include everyone you know who contributed to the post. Now, take a moment to consciously combat the negative messages in your life with constructive truths. Don't give up when you're not quick to find them. There is an actual truth for every negative message which will override the weight of despair. There are always those truths; keep looking until you find them.

You can get a negative message replaying in your mind if you make a mistake. You've been told as a child, "You're never going to amount to anything" or "You can't do anything right." When you make a mistake and you're going to because we all do - you can choose to overwrite that message with a positive one, such as "I choose to accept and grow from my mistake." or "As I learn from my mistakes, I become a better person." Good self-conversation isn't self-deception. It's not looking at circumstances mentally with eyes that just see what you want to see. Instead, positive self-talk is about acknowledging the truth in situations and within you. One of the fundamental truths is that you will be making mistakes. It is unfair to expect perfection in yourself or someone else. It's also unrealistic to expect no difficulties in life, whether by your own actions or by pure circumstances.

When adverse events or mistakes occur, positive self-talk is aimed at bringing the positive out of the negative in order to help you do better, go further or simply move forward. The practice of constructive self-talk is also the mechanism that helps you to discover in any given situation the hidden happiness, hope and joy.

# Conclusion

Once you accept that you are being manipulated, only then you can grasp the idea that you, "Yes, you," can do something about it. The concepts within this book will show you how to recognize the character traits of a manipulative person. Understanding what's happening to you is vital, so you can move on to the next stage of your life. Turn the pages and become a free person, under the influence of no-one but yourself.

We tend to believe manipulators must possess a certain degree of ruthlessness and don't feel sorry for the harm they cause their victims. This is the picture which is painted by movies and TV soap operas. But the reality is anyone can manipulate and persuade others, even the nicest people you know!

We are knowingly seeing dark psychological strategies in our daily lives. The manipulators secretly strike us, and we couldn't even know it. Manipulators use techniques in that matter, consciously. Some secret manipulators deliberately say and do stuff for influence and leverage to get what they want.

Using the information outlined in this book you can learn advanced persuasion strategies which are based upon human psychological loopholes and subconscious influencing.

Time to take a deep breath and assimilate all the information presented to you in this book.